To: [illegible]

Praying

And shou[illegible]

"You shine in the shadow of
His wings ~ He sees you when
others seem not too." May
your journey home to Him
be full of blessings!

Marie Therese Kreif
"Tammy"

MW00910972

Eve's Apple

a memoir

MARIE THERESE KCEIF

Inspiring Voices®

Copyright © 2014 Marie Therese Kceif.

All rights reserved. No part of this book may be used or reproduced by any means, graphic, electronic, or mechanical, including photocopying, recording, taping or by any information storage retrieval system without the written permission of the publisher except in the case of brief quotations embodied in critical articles and reviews.

Inspiring Voices books may be ordered through booksellers or by contacting:

Inspiring Voices
1663 Liberty Drive
Bloomington, IN 47403
www.inspiringvoices.com
1 (866) 697-5313

Because of the dynamic nature of the Internet, any web addresses or links contained in this book may have changed since publication and may no longer be valid. The views expressed in this work are solely those of the author and do not necessarily reflect the views of the publisher, and the publisher hereby disclaims any responsibility for them.

Disclaimer: This is my memoir. I have recreated it from my memory, documents, notes, journals and published news facts to tell the events and situations for over 30years of my life in the most accurate way possible. My recollections may not coincide with what others experienced or remember who are depicted in this memoir. Therefore, in consideration of that fact and in the interest of protecting identities and privacy, I have changed all names, relationships, cities, states, and other locations. Any resemblance to actual persons, living or dead, events, or locales is entirely coincidental."

Cover photography: Brad Hawks, Hicks Studio, 2545 West Silver Lake, Fenton MI 48430, all rights granted to author for the picture on the cover.

ISBN: 978-1-4624-1021-7 (sc)
ISBN: 978-1-4624-1023-1 (hc)
ISBN: 978-1-4624-1022-4 (e)

Library of Congress Control Number: 2014912897

Printed in the United States of America.

Inspiring Voices rev. date: 10/29/2014

Scripture quotations with NRSV annotation are from the New Revised Standard Version Bible: Catholic Edition, copyright © 1989, 1993 National Council of the Churches of Christ in the United States of America. Used by permission. All rights reserved.

Scripture quotations with RSVCE annotation are from the Revised Standard Version of the Bible—Second Catholic Edition (Ignatius Edition) Copyright © 2006 National Council of the Churches of Christ in the United States of America. Used by permission. All rights reserved.

Psalm 87 from the Grail Psalms Copyright © 1963, The Grail, England GIA Publications, Inc., exclusive North American agent, 7404 S. Mason Ave., Chicago, IL 60638 • www.giamusic.com • 800.442.1358 All rights reserved. Used by permission.

English translation of the *Catechism of the Catholic Church* for the United States of America, second edition copyright © 2001, United States Conference of Catholic Bishops—Libreria Editrice Vaticana. All rights reserved. Used by permission.

Encyclical letter by Pope Paul VI, *Humanae Vitae 14*, is quoted by the permission of: © Libreria Editrice Vaticana

God Calling and *God Calling II* edited by AJ Russell, OBooks & John Hunt Publishing LTD, Laurel House, Station Approach, Alresford, Hampshire SO249LH, in United States: Barbour Publishing, Inc. P.O. Box 719, 1810 Barbour Drive Uhrichsville, OH 44683, All rights reserved. Used by permission,

The English translation of the Non-Biblical Reading from *The Liturgy of the Hours* © 1973, 1974, 1975, International Commission on English in the Liturgy Corporation. Published with the approval of the Committee on Divine Worship, United States Conference of Catholic Bishops. All rights reserved. Used by permission.

Diary of Saint Maria Faustina Kowalska: Divine Mercy in My Soul ©1987, Marian Fathers of the Immaculate Conception of the B.V.M., All rights reserved. Used by permission.

S. J. Archives: Sacrifice Sacrament of the Holy Eucharist by Father John A. Hardon used by permission of Inter Mirifica. All rights reserved.

Printed With Ecclesiastical Permission. Most Reverend Earl Boyea. October 7, 2014. Nihil Obstat: Msgr Robert Lunsford, Censor Librorum. Imprimatur: ✠Most Reverend Earl Boyea, Bishop of Lansing.

To the saints of the Kingdom both here and in heaven; to all those who have helped form me for my final journey home.

Contents

Preface

*D*espite many harsh trials and much suffering, God opened my eyes to His loving guidance, ever-present love, and undeserved grace. This grace put a thirst in me for women's Bible studies, Christian spiritual retreats and conferences. At one such conference, we were prompted to put our journey of faith in writing so as to be considered as possible speakers for their conference.

I briefly wrote my story about how God pursued me as His daughter even though I was unfaithful to Him, showing me that He was alive in my life. Soon after that, I started to pray that God would use my story to help others see how near He was to them, too. Just then I was introduced to a retreat at our church called Christ Renews His Parish (CHRP) and through a spiritual discernment process I was chosen to give my witness. After that retreat, I was chosen to speak at our parish's mission during lent, and then the Bible study asked if I could also speak. Then the women's conference to which I had submitted my story asked me to speak in front of 1,500 women at their next conference. God was answering my prayer to be used to tell the story of my failures and His saving grace.

Over the years, many people had heard my story and had prompted me to write it down for others to read, but false humility and doubt kept me from starting the book. I truly wanted to glorify God, but every time I began to write, my words sounded selfish to me, not glorifying Him.

A friend of mine, Ralph Kuch, called and said he had been praying for me and had received a vision. In his vision I was sitting with blank sheets of paper and a pencil in my hand. Then he was brought forward to the future. I was much older and still at the same place with the blank white paper and pencil in hand. Then his vision brought me back to the age that I am now, but the story was written, and there were many hard cover books distributed to the many people who needed to hear it. Ralph told me he'd been shown that the book was the story of my life. Through Ralph, God was telling me to write my story and that I was procrastinating. So with the encouragement I needed, out of obedience, I started to write.

God has used me in powerful ways in speaking engagements and is using my story now through this book. "You are chosen …that you may declare the wonderful deeds of Him who called you out of darkness into His marvelous light" (1 Peter, 2:9 RSVCE).

I am humbled when I retell my story; every time I am amazed at how much God loves us even when we are unfaithful to Him. I am truly like Paul who stated in Ephesians 3:8, "I am the least of all of you," and like him, God has given me grace and a chance to use my life as a witness to His powerful love and forgiveness. He has given me a way back to Him. Now my only desire is to do His will, knowing through the retelling of my failures and His pursuit of me, He will use my story for good. My fervent desire is to be like Mary in my surrender: "Behold, I am the handmaid of the Lord; let it be to me according to your word" (Luke, 1:38 RSVCE). I have learned the joy, peace and love that come through obedience and holy surrender to His will in my life.

Every now and then I fail to be obedient, like Eve, reaching for apples of my own way or authority only to blame the serpent. But then I immerse myself in His presence and run back knowing He truly is my refuge. He truly is my Savior from my own failures. Now I know God is with me; Emmanuel, helping me to fight temptations, conquering in His power, and living for His glory. In this I have found great peace. "Thanks be to God through Jesus Christ our Lord! There is therefore now no condemnation for those who are in Christ Jesus. For those who live according to the Spirit set their minds on things of the Spirit . . .

to set the mind on the Spirit is life and peace" (Romans 7:25, 8:1, 5-6 RSVCE).

If you have this book in your hands, you can know surely that God is calling you to know His love more deeply and wants you, too, to be in His nestled arms of guidance, love, and security. You were chosen and loved by Him before you were even born. He wants you to know how special you are and how He has set you apart for a unique work that only you and Him together can do. He is waiting for your yes. "Before I formed you in the womb I knew you, and before you were born I consecrated you" (Jeremiah 1:5 RSVCE).

Introduction

Ever since I left the authority of my parent's home, I have been in a power and authority struggle with someone or other—military personnel, ex-husbands, even God himself. But the struggles have mainly been within me, thinking I was in charge and fighting anyone else who claimed to be, even if the fight was in my own mind. I have struggled for years to discern between healthy and unhealthy authority and then to act appropriately.

Growing up and working hard on a dairy farm in Wisconsin, my father was always the authority; I never questioned that, never argued with him. He was powerful, kind, and kept me safe. My mother taught us faith, introduced us to the Bible, and made sure we knew our prayers and went to mass every Sunday. When I was young, this clear, steadfast authority was enough for me. But when I moved away from home, I came to realize that I had free will to choose what I thought was right for myself, without counsel. For the most part up to that point I hadn't experienced unhealthy authority; thus, I didn't know how to discern between the two. So I lumped authority into one bundle and rejected most of it, good or bad.

I wanted to choose for myself. I chose a state college and a math major. I chose to stop praying and going to weekly mass and started having premarital sex. I chose the active duty army and married a man against my parents' advice. I chose, but I mistakenly thought that I had to tackle these big life decisions alone. It was almost as if I didn't want others to steal my freedom by helping to guide me.

In carefully guarding this newly found freewill, I cut off advice from my parents, the "stuffy" old church, and the ways of my heavenly Father. Somewhere along the line, I started to believe that it was weak to not make a solid decision autonomously. I became my own self-regulating government. I made the rules and became the definition of autonomous: "acting as a free and independent moral agent." ("autonomous.[dictionary](2007) In Microsoft Encarta(version2.1) [software] "Redmond, WA: Microsoft Corporation."") I thought I was my own best judge. I saw this self-sufficiency as strength, not realizing that it set me up for power struggles with all kinds of authority figures.

Though Socrates once said, "Know yourself"— I did not. Nor did I know my own limitations. God knew me way more than I knew myself. He gave me free will to choose Him and His way, but I kept turning away. So I plowed on for years, refusing the loving help of God the Father.

In the Bible, two women in particular were asked to use their free will to let God's authority save them and others they affected. Their given choices were both full of challenging circumstances. In the book of Genesis, Eve was given a choice to listen and follow God's will for her or choose her own way in the face of temptation. The Virgin Mary was also given a choice when God's holy messenger came to her asking if she would be the mother of God's only Son or to live life as a normal girl. One chose well; the other did not.

Though it looked hard and could even cause her death, Mary knew God's holy way was one of the Father's loving authority not just for the moment but for her future, and not just for her but for all involved. Her "Yes" to God led to the salvation of the world. Eve, on the other hand, chose the purported promises offered by the father of lies rather than God's truths, and this choice led to her exile from the garden and left the rest of the world to struggle with the temptation of sin. Both of their choices affected everyone around them for generations to come.

I was like Eve, turning to my own free will, choosing the worldly promises of excitement, autonomy, pleasure and reward not considering nor believing how it could affect other people around me for generations to come. Like Eve, I said yes to Satan's lies because I allowed myself to be distant from Christ's presence though He was always near. "And He made from one, every nation of men to live on all the face of the earth, having determined allotted periods and the boundaries of their habitation, that they should seek God, in the hope that they might feel after him and find him. Yet he is not far from each one of us" (Acts 17:26-27 RSVCE). My choice to not seek Him when making the decisions of my life left me without peace, hope, or love, even for myself.

"But where sin increased, grace abounded all the more," (Romans 5:20, RSVCE). God came and scooped me up out of the pit and gave me a second chance, in fact, many second chances. I am learning to become more like the New Testament Eve; Mary, because I am learning from her to be surrendered in my own "yes" to accepting His Way, Truth and Life; Jesus, and the grace of His cross even when it pierces my own heart. There is no one who has sinned too far, rebelled against His loving authority too much or affected others so badly that His saving power can't reach. "When the disciples heard this they were greatly astonished, saying, "Who then can be saved?" But Jesus looked at them and said to them, "With men this is impossible, but with God all things are possible."." (Matthew19:25-26 RSVCE). Thanks be to God for His Amazing Grace!

CHAPTER 1

The Apple of Self-sufficiency, Pride, and Worldly Power

"Let him who is without sin among you be the first to throw a stone at her." (John8:7 RSVCE) I too was down in the sand saved by the stones dropping one by one as Jesus protected His beloved. Let me take you back to the time before this woman's adultery was found out, before Eve picked her apple, before the woman at the well married her five husbands; back to the how and why we find ourselves down in the sand humbled in our sin. Come with me on my journey full of choices that led me to such sorrow and yet how much Jesus pursued, loved and forgave His own—bringing His precious bride to the wedding feast; ready, pure, surrendered; forgiven.

College time was a time before my "humbled sand" days. These were youthful days full of shinny apples—good things, but none the less, things I was not ready to have or not in God's will or timing for my life. But like many, I had not learned to ask God for His will for my choices, to wait on His guidance and plunged into the picking of fruit not ripe or allowed as good for me. "Trust in the LORD with all your heart, and do not rely on your own insight. In all your ways acknowledge

1

Him, and He will make straight your paths. Be not wise in your own eyes; fear the LORD, and turn away from evil. It will be healing to your flesh* and refreshment* to your bones."(Pvb3:5-8, RSVCE) Back in college I did not understand the "fear of the Lord" and what that meant played out in my choices.

One of the first choices I was presented with in college through Army ROTC (Reserve Officer Training Corp) was a slot in the active duty Army Aviation Branch via flight school. The choice was an easy one for me, but often in my life it is not the choice that gets me in trouble so much as how I live out the choice and why I made the choice in the first place. The big lie of the serpent in my personal garden has been that self glory will lead to all kinds of great joyful adventures. Unlike Mordecai in the book of Esther, I did not choose to act out of honor for God but rather for self. "But I did this that I might not set the glory of man above the glory of God, and I will not bow down to anyone but to Thee, who art my Lord; and I will not do these things in pride."(Ester13:14, RSVCE) Unlike Mordecai, I bowed down to self-glory. Life can be so full of security and rich joy; complete joy, if we are in and for the will of God and His glory. But in my self-absorbsion I pushed on to possess this slot in flight school for my own glory and adventure, not His.

A coveted slot as a commissioned officer in the United States Army Aviation Flight School is neither for the lukewarm nor even for high achievers. It is for the champions, the best of the best. The words *couldn't*, *impossible*, and even *maybe* were not in my vocabulary, though there were near unsurpassable hurdles to overcome for me and for the hundreds who tried to qualify. To be considered as a candidate for flight school meant exceeding many requirements. One must have a score of ninety percent or higher on the FAST Test (Flight Aptitude Selection Test), which includes questions about pulleys, minor mechanics, and math. The candidate must also successfully pass a Class 1A FDME (Flying Duty Medical Exam) that requires being in top medical condition. This includes 20/20 vision and being able to handle a high altitude chamber, among other things. Another requirement is to excel on an Army Physical Fitness test (AFPT test). This test includes a timed two-mile run, a two-minute sit-up test, and a two-minute pushup test, all done consecutively as one comprehensive test. For so many in my school trying to compete for the two spots available, we had to rise above the others on this test as well.

For my age group of twenty-two in 1988, the women's maximum fitness score to meet the requirement of excelling for flight school would mean doing at least; fifty-six pushups in two minutes, eighty-five sit-ups in two minutes, and running two miles in 15:36 minutes consecutively. The men's maximum score would mean: eighty pushups in two minutes, eighty-seven sit-ups in two minutes, and running the two mile in 12:36 minutes(Standards from: DA Form 705 May 87). I scored one 110 pushups, 110 sit-ups and ran the two mile in 12:50 minutes.

In the college I attended, the candidate also had to have a Bachelors of Science in a subject such as mathematics, engineering, or science. To top it off, your commanding officer had to recommend you. Only two candidates at our state university (enrollment of 9,300 students) were awarded a slot each year. Clearly, you had to be qualified, but moreover, you had to desire it with your very being. These were the qualifications that I not only met, but exceeded.

In college, I proved myself to be fiercely competitive, driven, capable, and strong-willed — perfect Army Aviation Commissioned Officer material. I was five feet six-and-three-quarter inches, 115 pounds, and full of youthful vigor and self-reliance — a real go-getter. I packed my schedule, not wanting to lose any opportunity that might knock on my door.

Having grown up on an old north Midwestern 120-acre dairy farm, I was accustomed to demanding physical labor and multitasking, but being a farm girl also meant I was without extra money. This meant I had to work during college to make ends meet. I took a job at a fitness center, about one-and-a-half miles from my dorm room, where I was a lifeguard, water aerobics instructor, front desk coordinator, and towel washer. In addition, I decided to go out for ROTC to help pay for college and fulfill my lifelong desire to travel and see the world.

Because I'd been an honors student my whole life, my advisor set me up with twenty-two credits my first semester, a heavy academic load by any standard. On top of all this, I changed my major from wildlife management to mathematics in my second year. In addition to my heavy academic load I was also in ballet classes, raced as a member of the United States Cycling Federation (USCF), belonged to the Reserve Officer Training Corp (ROTC), competed on the university swim team, had a boyfriend, and worked about fifteen hours a week.

My daily schedule went something like this: wake up at 5:00 am, go to a two-hour swim practice, do the ROTC fitness workout (a run with pushups and sit-ups), attend a strenuous ballet class and academic classes, squeeze in a late lunch or early supper, attend a second afternoon swim practice with weight training, run to work (I didn't have a car), and then run back to my dorm to study or see my boyfriend. I usually had a night class, and if I could find time, I squeezed in bike training.

As a result my grades suffered, the Catholic faith I'd been raised in was forced to take a back seat, and my body became anemic due to inadequate nutrition and too much activity. It never occurred to me that I couldn't do it all. I just thought I had to try harder. This steel-willed determination was why I was awarded one of the only two slots in our state university for flight school in the U.S. Army. The drive to achieve and be the best was strong and possibly good in itself, but it was not coupled with a drive to be at peace within, with God, and with others. It could not be sustained for long.

God, the Great I AM, thinks *being* is so important that His very name means *being*. And the army thinks it's so important that their motto is, "*Be* all you can *be*," not "*Do* all you can *do*." Like Martha (Luke 10: 41-42), I needed to learn how crucial letting my actions flow from being with the Great "I AM" was for making healthy decisions. I didn't even think that was important at the time. "To conquer adverse circumstances, conquer yourselves. The answer to the desire of My Disciples to follow Me was 'Be ye therefore perfect, even as your Father which is in heaven is perfect.' To accomplish much, be much. In all cases the doing, to be well-doing, must be the mere unconscious expression of the being."(*God Calling*, May 2, edited by AJ Russell) Despite my qualifications and strong will, my lack of humility toward God in thinking I needed His wisdom and presence, not only weakened me as a leader but brought me the most profound suffering I've ever known. But I was too blind to see it then, even when it was plastered everywhere as the army's motto!

Doing should flow from being, if my being was all about me, how could I sustain? I now see that I was in a power struggle with God's healthy authority over mine, like Eve not wanting God's guidance but deciding to follow her own authority to eat the apple. The youthful vigor described in the book of Job, "His bones are full of youthful vigor, but it will lie down with him in the dust" (Job 20:11, RSVCE) eventually weighed down my soul and tired it out until something like a death eventually set in. Though He was gently trying to show me how to be my best in His way for His glory, I was trying to be my best in my own way for my glory.

In addition to going to flight school right after graduation, I was stubbornly determined to marry my boyfriend, Jason, so that we could have this big adventure together, even though it was against my parents' wishes. I met Jason one afternoon when I was a freshman lifeguarding at the college pool when he and his younger brother came to get in shape for the university swim team's season. We instantly made a connection, and Jason suggested that I compete for the swim team.

I had never been on a swim team in my life. Our small farming community didn't have the funds to put in a pool. My closest connection with swimming was being a lifeguard and a WSI (Water Safety Instructor) at our small hometown's river beach, but Jason's easy, persuasive, encouraging tones piqued my curiosity. Farm life hadn't fully given me the chance to really compete in the sports like I had wanted to, but it had given me the physical strength I needed. I had never dreamed of actually being on a college sports team, much less a swim team!

Soon Jason had me working out in the pool and was teaching me to do flip turns and competitive strokes. When I asked the coach for the chance to tryout, I told her that I'd be the hardest worker she'd ever have. With Coach Fotig's grace, Jason's encouragement, and my determination, I not only made the team but lettered the last three years I competed.

When we started dating, Jason was always encouraging me to try new things, strive harder, and "*Be* all that I could *be*," only that meant to us both, *do* all we could *do*. He was a tall man, thin but muscular, having one of the lowest fat percentages I ever knew possible. He also got me into bicycle racing and healthful eating. Like me, Jason was driven with youthful vigor, having graduated with a double major in political science and communications. He, too, had put his faith and internal growth in Christ on the back burner, clouding it with the quest for temporal perfection. He was constantly working out, studying, and trying to improve his physical self. Together we were quite a pair.

He was raised Catholic in a small rural Midwestern suburb. But like me Jason had stopped frequenting church letting his faith lapse in place of other pursuits. His father was a happy, easy going sweet man while his mother was more serious focusing on strong morals and rules. Jason did not like much physical display of affection. For example, he didn't like holding hands, receiving that small rub on the upper part of your back, or anything like that. And his mother made it clear that she did not want any hand holding when we went to visit them, went to a store, or if they came to visit.

I was different. I felt loved by having my hand held, like someone was proud to be with me, especially since we had the intimacy of premarital sex. We were both raised that premarital sex was wrong but had decided that our desires and our belief that we had found "the one" justified our decision. But it didn't relieve our consciences. I believe that Jason's lack of affection toward me was his way of expressing his guilty conscience over rejecting church authority on premarital sex, not knowing if he really loved me, and his mother's harsh prohibition on any displays of affection. I didn't see the connection or the need to hide my affection. I only knew it hurt when he dropped my hand in company.

This difference caused us problems in our relationship over time and was something we should have taken seriously and addressed early on. Instead, we drove that difference into hiding, possibly not wanting to face the truth or show weakness. We dated all four of my college years, and as soon as I received the slot for flight school, we got married — August 27, 1988.

Jason was one year ahead of me so he had to wait until I graduated. He hadn't had much luck getting a job in his major in the local area, and knowing we were to leave for active duty in the army, I don't think he pursued it with much zeal. After being let go from an office job, he focused on his bicycle racing and odd jobs like busing tables for the year he waited for us to go. Being on active duty meant moving every three years or more, which did not encourage him to pursue a career, but to support me, find jobs wherever we went, and fit in the best he could. Both of our parents tried to counsel us that this would be a problem. We should have taken heed to it, but we thought we could overcome it. We would do it our way with or without their full blessing.

Before I knew it, I had graduated from Airborne School in August of '88 (parachute school), Officers' Basic Course in August of '89, Air Assault School in September of '89 (repelling from aircraft school) and Flight School in July of '90 with the top physical fitness award in all schools. I was ready! I was stationed in Central Europe in July of 1990 as a new second lieutenant and platoon leader with my new husband and a demanding career as an army pilot.

United States army officers who were pilots were divided into two rank categories: traditional commissioned officers (me) and warrant officers (the pilots I would be leading). Back in 1990, the warrant officer could be chosen right from high school to attend flight school. He or she just had to meet all the above requirements minus the degree, which later changed to a requirement of two years of college, or he or she could be a noncommissioned officer, in other words, a sergeant or higher who applied for the rank of warrant officer and fulfilled all the requirements to go to flight school. Warrant officers' ranks progressed from warrant officer one (WO1), chief warrant officer two (CW2) and so on up to CW5.

The warrant officer's job was to be the pilot in command, the technical expert in the aircraft, and a proficient flyer so that the unit's leader, and also pilot with rank of 2LT and above, could focus on leading the mission while still flying. Traditional commissioned officer ranks started at second lieutenant (2LT), progressed to first lieutenant (1LT), captain (CPT), major, lieutenant colonel, full bird colonel, then on to the star ranks. As a 2LT, I was young and just coming in from flight school fresh and full of vigor, raring to go all the way. I immersed myself into my career with everything I had. Though I had been raised a devout Catholic knowing the importance of marriage, I had left little time for Jason, let alone God.

Stationed in Central Europe, I was leading a platoon and flying generals for the V Corps. As a platoon leader, one of the first things I did was to fly along as a passenger on some of my pilots' flights. This gave me the experience of watching the others fly without the pressure of being on the controls and also helped me to get to know the pilots who worked for me. Our pilots often had power struggles while flying together, especially if they were full of youthful pride and vigor — as most of our CW2 pilots were. Usually by the rank of CW2, pilots have also made PIC (Pilot in Command), which is to say they have mastered the aircraft. If a pilot has PIC status, he or she can log PIC time while flying, which means they take full responsibility for the flight, or just log in as copilot if they are flying with another PIC. The crew; the two pilots, determines who will be the PIC before takeoff if both have made that status; both cannot log PIC at the same time. Someone has to be in charge. If this decision isn't made ahead of time, it can be a set up for a power struggle of who's in charge and cause confusion and accidents.

Once I decided as a new 2LT to go along as a passenger on a training flight with two CW2s, both of whom had PIC status. They were both full of pride and showing off, lacking the confident humility that comes with age. We soon got into a situation with low visibility. Having the doors open in the back, both the crew chief and I saw just how dangerous our lack of visibility had become. Bumping the aircraft around in the air, the two pilots started to argue over who was calling the shots, even though they had already decided who was logging copilot time and who was logging PIC time before takeoff. The pilot logging copilot time was not humble enough to let the other pilot actually *be* the PIC, and the pilot logging PIC wasn't humble enough to take the other's advice. Though they had decided who had the authority, they hadn't truly subscribed to it in their heart.

The crew chief looked at me as if to say, "Are you going to do something?" I keyed the mic and said, "Hey, guys, this is getting dangerous." It was all I had to say. They took the aircraft in but not without arguing all the way back. From that day forward, I took personalities into consideration when deciding who would fly with whom. That experience showed me a valuable lesson about crew selection, but it showed me how pride has the potential to destroy a journey, even a life journey. Both of those pilots had excellent flying skills and knowledge of the aircraft, but they lacked humility, balance, and a vision of the bigger picture. Perhaps God was trying to give me a spiritual lesson in a tangible way but unfortunately I didn't get the lesson until I was more humble, mature, and balanced myself. Many times in my life God gives me foreshadows of mistakes to learn from before I make them myself... if I am humble with open heart I see them for my own learning, but many times I miss them altogether.

After a year of being a platoon leader and 2LT flying the V Corps generals around Central Europe, on April 30, 1991, I received the next rank of 1LT and was offered a coveted position that would be very advantageous to my career. The military had developed what was known as Allied Mobile Forces (AMF). This mission was a small NATO reaction force designed to show solidarity with our members against aggressing nations in the bordering countries of Europe. It was early 1991, and we were still being careful not to fly into demilitarized zones (DMZs) or No Fly Zones in East Germany, Northern Korea, or Russia. The fact that the wall between East and West Germany had just come down in late 1989 and reunification hadn't happened until late 1990, the atmosphere of anticipation was heightened in Europe. Thousands of Russian troops were still in their military complexes in East Germany and they were not to be provoked. In general, people were on edge. Other areas were heating up such as Croatia, its first shots being fired in April of 1991, the Iraq Gulf War starting in August 1990 to which half of our unit was already deployed, and the unrest that had already started in Somalia. Times were uncertain and fluid for us in Europe.

Being in the land portion (AMF-L), the United States, our unit, and ultimately myself, had been selected that year to lead a small section of UH1-H (Huey) helicopters to fly the dignitaries and generals around the battlefield for meetings and information reconnaissance flights all over Europe. For instance, I would take the train alone up to Denmark, meet with the British Information Officer, usually a Colonel, receive specific orders and maps, plan out our strategy with him, come back to my unit, brief my group, and then redeploy back to Denmark to set up camp. Many of these higher ranked officers, always male, were uncomfortable that the US had sent a female and a lowly 1Lt at that. One British colonel actually asked me if there was someone else coming. It was a bit intimidating, but it was exactly what I thrived on — challenge. I would then come back to my unit to brief, get their advice and suggestions, then deploy the group of helicopters, pilots, and supplies up to Denmark and set up with the German pilots out in the field next to the British and French pilots according to the plans.

Once we arrived on site, we hit the ground running, actually flying nonstop missions day and night. We were given exciting missions like flying the prince of Belgium and a five-star General of the German Army and being backup flight support of the fly in for the Queen of Denmark. We looked down on fiords and castles with moats and watched as waves crashed upon the shoreline of bluffs while we flew by. It was an experience of a lifetime.

I even had the opportunity to fill the copilot slot on foreign aircraft, flying German dual engine Hueys, Pumas, and Gazelles. The Puma belonged to the French section camped out near us and was being used to do air assault missions with French soldiers repelling out of its belly as we hovered overhead. Having been through our U.S. Air Assault training, I was really excited to be able to pilot such soldiers. In fact, I loved it. The Gazelles, owned by the British, were camped out in an old barn near our site. They were used as a lightweight utility and/or reconnaissance helicopter. The German version of the American UH-1 had two engines instead of our one, and also had a blade stop, which we didn't have. Duel engine time is what really counts outside the army if you want a job with the airlines. It's expensive to achieve on your own but free in the military, so pilots love racking up duel engine time if they can get it. Plus if one engine dies, you still have another one to keep you running in the air. The blade stop they had helped stop blades faster during shutdown, so you could put the aircraft away more efficiently instead of waiting for the engine to wind down and the blades to stop on their own. Needless to say, working with these choppers was a privilege.

All three types of aircraft had two pilot seats, one for the PIC and the other for a copilot. Many of the Puma and Gazelle pilots didn't want to fill the copilot slot because being less than PIC wounded their pride. Lieutenant rank and above leads the group and is in charge of the battle, but the PIC is in charge of flying the aircraft safely and efficiently, thereby allowing the leader to stay focused on battle decisions while flying. Usually, but not always, the PIC is not the leader because it would be too much to handle all at once. So normally the leader logs copilot time while flying and leading the battle. But for two warrant officers to fly together who are not leading means that the copilot is taking a step down in responsibility because they do not have the overall battle decisions to worry about.

Taking the copilot slot did not take away my rank. It was all still flying to me — plus flying foreign aircraft with foreign pilots — what an experience! The foreign pilots welcomed a female American pilot in this open seat, as they didn't see many of us. Actually, I was the only one in the whole area. This made for a more interesting mission, and I jumped at the chance.

Though I had abandoned God for the most part during this time in my life, God had not abandoned me. I put God to the test one stormy night in Denmark when I accepted a mission against my better judgment. It was the first of many times in the military that I experienced the miracle of God's protection despite my rebellion.

We had been flying non-stop, watching our crew rest and aircraft's hours for phase and being rather creative to fulfill our requirements and still be able to do our mission. Phase is the block of hours an aircraft can fly before it goes into maintenance for about a month for a real good look over. Crew rest is the same for pilots; we can only legally fly a certain number of hours before we need to take off for a set number of hours. It was the Army's way of acknowledging needed "Mary" (Luke 10: 41-42) time. We all hated crew rest rules and tried to finagle ways to fly more, but the military authority knew that it would keep the pilots attentive and the aircraft and crew safe.

The five-star German general, radioed in a mission to our Tactical Operations Center (a tent with secure radio communications set up with a flight planning table) for us to fly him to a remote, top-secret meeting place in the woods somewhere about an hour away. He said the mission was urgent. The visibility was at the lowest legal limit, possibly even below it. We did have a brand-new Geographic Positioning System (GPS), though we were not fully trained in how to use it. It was a big black box back then and not as reliable as ours today. Our crew rest limit was so close that we had a good chance of breaking it on the way back if we didn't find the place right away and come back without a hitch.

As the commander of our little section, it was up to me to decide whether or not to comply with the mission . . . and the general was pushing hard. The general was a hard man, or at least that is what he led us to believe. He didn't speak but three or four words the entire time. I was only a 1LT at the time, making the decision even more intimidating, so I talked it over with the other CW2 pilot, Gawner, who flew for me in the platoon and who also had enough crew rest left. Gawner said that he would do the flying but that it was my responsibility to navigate because he wasn't going to take the rap for getting a five-star general of the German army lost in Denmark in the middle of the night in bad weather. I decided it was a fair agreement. We wired over that we would be ready to go in 15 minutes.

God knew I needed Gawner that night. He was a good, calm pilot with faith. I think he must have prayed that night for both of us because it was a miracle that we found the sight and made it through alive. Soon after we did our pre-flight on the helicopter, and the crew chief was settled in the back, a light, misty rain started to come down. We picked up the general and started to fly.

Flying in Denmark is dangerous, especially at night, because of the windmills and the high-tension wires. Many of them are not on the map. We had marked most of them during reconnaissance flights, but many of the small, local wires were not on our maps. We had to fly the general into a remote wooded spot that was top secret, which meant the ground soldiers would not be out with their flashlights for an inverted Y to fly toward until after we actually started an approach. We had to be dead on with our navigation to the exact tree line and spot. Our GPS wasn't working, so we had to go on our own navigations. It was especially stressful in the cockpit because the general had plugged himself in and could listen to our conversation, which went something like this.

"Wires in five kilometers, three, two, one, 500 meters, come up," I said. Then we would see the wires and pop up, over, and back down to NOE. (Nap of the earth (NOE) is flying at tree top level and sometimes just below to avoid detection or attack from the enemy.)

"Visibility low," I said, "but there should be a windmill off to your left, in one kilometer, 500 meters, two, one . . . come right. Correct."

"Good job, Lieutenant. You on?" said Gawner, shooting me a look as if to tell me that he was definitely lost and could not help.

"We're on," I shot back, but inside I was just not sure. Not sure with the rain, the blackness of the moonless, cloud covered night, the sickness in the pit of my stomach that came with knowing we could hit a wire or windmill if I wasn't absolutely sure, or if I missed something on the map.

Soon we came upon a wooded area connected to a field. This was where my navigation and plotting of the grid coordinates had placed us. In the darkness, it all looked the same. There were many wooded areas with fields coming up to them. If I was off by one field, no one would come out to signal us in. What would the general do if we were lost and couldn't get him to his meeting?

"We are within one kilometer," I told Gawner.

He looked over at me with fear-filled, wondering eyes, as if to say "You sure, Lieutenant?"

The windshield wipers of our old helicopter swapped back and forth in the silence as I smiled a weak smile that told him I wasn't one hundred percent sure, but it had better be right, or we were in trouble.

"Ok, field to 030 degrees at 500 meters, shoot approach," I announced. We started the approach, and just as we were about 200 feet above the ground, out came the flashlights and the soldiers to guide us in. *Relief!*

From the back, in his German accent, the general spoke into the intercom. "Good flying, good job, and thank you for getting me here under such conditions." As soon as we landed, he gave a quick salute, ran out our open doors into the woods, and we were waved off.

On the way back, we were yelling in the cockpit, "Yahoo!" and "Wooh!" and "I can't believe we found it!" I don't think the general thought he was going to make his meeting that night either. It was still stressful on the way back but not as bad because we were able to speak freely. We discussed how it was a miracle, a pure miracle, that we were alive and had found that field site. I even decided on the way back that there would be no more marginal flights no matter what was going on.

But something that day stayed with me deeply. It was the knowing that God was with me, not just a feeling, but a real knowing that He had guided my hand on that map and that that was the only reason we had found our goal. I knew without a doubt it was Him. Strange for me then to know this because I hadn't had much faith or a knowing of His presence before that, but I knew it that night every time we came up to a telephone wire or a windmill that I had seen though it wasn't necessarily on our maps. "If we are faithless, he remains faithful—for He cannot deny Himself."(2Tim3:13 RSVCE) It was God showing me He had not abandoned me.

Although it didn't change my life that night, though maybe it should have, it was a seed of faith that stayed with me for years that reminded me He was real, very real. Thank You, God, for Your undying love for us even when we fly away from You and Your ways. Like St. Augustine in *Confessions* said, "When I first came to know you, you drew me to yourself so that I might see that there were things for me to see, but that I myself was not yet ready to see them. Meanwhile you overcame the weakness of my vision, sending forth most strongly the beams of your light, and I trembled at once with love and dread. I learned that I was in a region unlike yours and far distant from you, and I thought I heard your voice from on high… Late have I loved you, O Beauty, ever ancient, ever new, late have I loved you! You were within me, but I was outside, and it was there that I searched for you. In my unloveliness, I plunged into the lovely things that you created. You were with me, but I was not with you. Created things kept me from you; yet if they had not been in you, they would not have been at all. You called, you shouted, and you broke through my deafness. You flashed, you shone, and you dispelled my blindness. You breathed your fragrance on me; I drew in breath, and now I pant for you. I have tasted you, now I hunger and thirst for more. You touched me, and I burned for your peace." (Memorial of St Augustine, 2nd reading from The English translation of the Non-Biblical Reading from *The Liturgy of the Hours*) Like Augustine, I, too, did not know God, but He pursued me through those years of leaving Him, and He was never far away. I ran for some years from His presence, but Denmark was always deep inside me, tapping me on the shoulder; reminding me of His call.

Not long after Denmark, I was moved to the Class III/V platoon (fuel and ammo), which was part of the S4 logistics group of our unit.

We received orders to draw down our airfield and move our base about 1.5 hours southeast to a small old German WWII aircraft base with small village type buildings, tall, old trees, and an outside public pool. Deactivation of the old base took forty-five days and most of my time. During that time Jason lived near the new post while I was running back and forth between posts. When we finally got settled I was deployed again to Caravan Guard and Reforger 1992 from the September 8 to October 9. It seemed the active duty would keep me deployed either with training for AMF(L) to Italy, Denmark, or working in the field as an S4 logistics at Caravan Guard or Reforger. I was away from our home more than I was there.

In Denmark, we all got away one night and went to the local town to have a drink and hang out. I was always around men, and this became normal to me. When I got back from Denmark and went to Caravan Guard and Reforger the same kind of stuff happened. I would "innocently" go out for a drink after work with the guys while deployed.

After I got back from deployment of Reforger, I was home alone because Jason had gone on a week-long bicycling trip. The unit put on a dance for the small post where we were, so I decided to go. Everyone was dancing, and I loved to dance.

An officer a little older than me from outside our unit came over and asked me if I wanted to dance, and without thinking, I said yes. I didn't see that he had ulterior motives; I just wanted to have fun and feel the youthful freedom of the beat under my feet. The commander of our headquarters group who was a Captain, and who'd recently went through a divorce himself for reasons of adultery, was watching over me without my knowledge. He must have seen my ignorance and known of this older officer's reputation. He came over to us and said to the officer, "Sorry, you'll need to leave her alone, she's married. Come on, Lieutenant, come over and sit down with us." I listened to him because I respected him and knew that if he had gone to the trouble of saying something it would be worth listening to. It was nice of him. He cared about my marriage, even when I wasn't looking out for it myself. God sends us little helps along the way even when we aren't aware we need it.

In late November 1992, the colonel of our unit came down to my office one afternoon and I sprung to attention. He stated, "Your former boss, the S4, was fired this morning, and you will be taking his place. And by the way, we just received orders that we will be deploying a task force of 700 people to Somalia in support of a mission called 'Operation Restore Hope.' You will be the new S4 of it. We leave in 2 weeks. Do you think you are up to the challenge?"

"Yes, sir!" I replied feeling ready for a challenge, but somehow a bit worried if I could do it. He turned from the room and left. It was like that during my European time, from one thing right into the other. We never had down time, never a time to breathe. But I liked that kind of life style. It was what I had gotten used to in college. Not that it was healthy for me, my faith, or my marriage, but that is probably why I liked it. It allowed me to numb myself to any problems.

God gave me a chance not to go, but I stubbornly drove on. There was another lieutenant who would have been a better choice to go as the S4 after I got the unit prepared for deployment. He was in charge of accounting for all the equipment in our unit and worked under me in my S4 group. He came to ask me if he could go instead of me and stated why he thought it would be best. He was right, but I told him no. I wanted the status, the combat patch, the time away, and the adventure. He knew how to run the special field computer used to account for all the equipment in all our units. I was in charge of the S4 but didn't possess this needed ability. I told him he could do that function back at our home base as we communicated back to him.

Now writing this, it didn't make sense. He could have learned the supply lines like I did while in Somalia and run his counts while deployed. He'd have been closer to the equipment to get a truer count. I could have pushed things to their sector as needed and watched over the units we had back in the rear. This decision wasn't for the better of the whole or for God's glory but for my own. The real reasons I wanted to go were that I didn't want to do all the work of getting the unit deployed without going with them, which ultimately was self-glory and also I didn't want to have to stay behind with Jason.

I remember sitting on the top of the stairs of our rental property the night before deploying for Somalia. My bags were packed, and I was on the precipice of embarking on a new life experience, which should have thrilled me. But some of His truth was in me, lingering, as if to tell me this was going to change my life drastically and possibly in ways that would not be altogether good for me or my marriage. God was still calling me, like in Denmark. Suddenly, I wanted to quit the army, I wanted Jason to have a job, I wanted to be pregnant and be a stay-at-home mom living in a small community with security. I wanted my life as it was to just . . . disappear. For a moment, I actually wanted the other lieutenant to go but knew it was too late. I felt the weight of the world on my shoulders as never before. I knew in part it was the eighteen to twenty hour days I'd been having as the logistics officer, preparing the Task Force for deployment with only two weeks' notice, but it was more. I knew I was about to turn a page in my life that would affect me forever.

I had that feeling something wrong was about to happen, as if I sensed a turn for the worst. Somalia. The children's bloated stomachs as they looked at me with their fly-caked eyes crying for *wa wa*, the starving people, the man who said he'd marry me if I gave him my boots, the strong, sweet yet putrid smell of decaying flesh as they threw yet another dead body over the parapet to decay in the open air, the dead bloated donkey laying in the round-about as we drove by in the center of Mogadishu next to the boy laying by it almost dead himself, the war lords' uncaring control over the starving — these images are all still in my memory of those days.

Somalia was an austere environment, especially in Baledogal; the abandoned airstrip in which we were deployed, two hours in from the coast and Mogadishu. We were based out of an old Turkish, run down, bombed out airport with no electricity or running water. There were no hard floors either, except for one abandoned building we used as our headquarters and office. Other than that one building and the rugged runway, there was just sand, sand and more sand.

In the middle of our campsite, we built a wooden hut that was three-and-a-half feet square by seven feet tall, just big enough for one person to stand in a big plastic bowl with a ladle. We washed in this with our small amount of rationed water so we wouldn't lose a drop. If you were smart, you even brought your laundry to wash after you were done. One day, one of our female soldiers was in there trying to wash up, and a scorpion came into the water with her. She ran out screaming, stark naked.

We slept in tents with wood we brought from home called oriented strand board (OSB), which was like particle board for the floors. But because there were termite hills everywhere you looked, they ate the wood right out from under us. Once a Camel Spider, a really big, brown, furry thing with large legs got into our tent. I came back to the tent one afternoon to hear the two girls I shared the tent with screaming. They were standing on their cots while the camel spider walked around in the middle of the tent. I chuckled at them but thought, "Did that camel spider come in here when I was sleeping? Did it crawl over me without me knowing?"

We ate dehydrated foods in plastic pouches, basically survival food, called "meals ready to eat" (MRE) for breakfast, lunch, and supper for the first two months. The temperatures ran an average of 103 degrees Fahrenheit daily. We'd wash our clothes and in just seconds they'd be a burnt orange color from the blowing sand. Somalia was not your Hawaiian vacation spot.

This austere environment made me feel even tougher than the others. It reminded me of my old farm days; milking the cows at 4:30 am before school, throwing the forty pound hay bales up in the hay loft sweating in the hot humid barn during summer hay season, cutting wood for the furnace out in the woods and working in the fields. I figured that most other soldiers, especially the women, probably hadn't ever experienced tough times, but I had. We were poor. I had eaten canned food from the garden and meat we had butchered ourselves my whole life. I had planted and picked cucumbers to sell for pickling that helped to buy our school clothes. Somalia was more of an adventure to me than a hardship. Instead of feeling sorry for those who were whining, wanting the pleasures of home, I felt superior to them. In fact, it made things even more exciting and adventurous. I shrugged them off as immature, pampered people who weren't taking into consideration how their upbringing may have affected them. I thought they had to learn how to get tough like I had, like developing a callous on a worker's hand over time.

In my pride filled judgment of others, I hadn't realized many of them came into the military out of inner city poverty. Some of the women had experienced the pain of childbirth, which I hadn't;

some had been through emotional distress, abuse, and abandonment, which I hadn't. Most of them had learned it was ok to reach out to one another in weakness so that the whole would be stronger and act more like a strong, cohesive family. But I set myself above this family, above wanting to know personal weakness though it was deep within me.

One day, I was assigned to lead a ground convoy to Mogadishu. We had to go to the port and pick up two UH60 fuel blivots; 450-gallon external fuel tanks, and bring them back to put on the aircraft. To an untrained eye, these external fuel tanks looked like rockets.

Finally, after a long, dusty haul with camels running alongside us, and nothing but sand for miles and miles while maneuvering through the dangers of Mogadishu, we got into Somalia's theater of war and a more permanent port area of operations on the coast, which we called a cantonment area. The airport, hospital, and logistics operations home base was contained within its high walls separating it from the town of Mogadishu. Being within the confines of "friendlies" or Allied Forces kept it mostly safe from warlords.

I went up to the logistics office to get permission to load up the fuel tanks from the commanding S4 who was a colonel. I dusted myself off the best I could and went into the office. My salute was returned with a smug, disdainful look and the words, "Lieutenant, where did you come from looking like that?" I told him we were from Baledogal and that we had to make it back before nightfall. The whole office, dressed in clean fatigues, just stared at us with our flack vests and sand-filled boots and uniforms. Soon we had lots of help and were loaded up for the trip back but not before we got a good meal at their chow hall and went to the shore near the port to go swimming in the ocean while pulling parameter duty. This involved putting a few soldiers on watch while the others swam. This area of swimming was not fully in the confines of the safely guarded port but just on its edge.

We had been rationed a helmet of water a day for washing. Not having had a shower for months, I could scarcely say no to the group. I made them all promise to keep it a secret, or it could mean my job. (Later, after we'd been back for a while, the operations officer who was a major mentioned to me how nice it would be to go to the shore for a swim. He said this with a knowing smile and a pat on the back. He also realized that morale had been lifted because of that little swim, but left it in the realm of the unspoken.)

On the way back from Mogadishu, we ran into trouble outside the safety of the gate. Warlords had control of the whole area. They set up ambushes to confiscate anything that looked useful. Before we left, I had watched the city below from the top of a building within the confines of the port and actually witnessed such an ambush. They were stealing grain out of one of the U.S. trucks we had sent out to feed the starving citizens of the city. It was if I was being forewarned that it could happen to us. So when we left the cantonment area, we traveled with the Heavily Expanded Mobility Tactical Truck (HEMMT) Wrecker, a ten-ton, eight-wheeled recovery truck with a winch and a crane in front because it was capable of plowing through obstacles if needed. I was the leader of the convoy but placed myself behind the third vehicle so that I could watch the convoy. I also placed a five-ton cargo truck behind us, last in the convoy.

Before we left, we zipped the doors off because the temperatures were hovering around 105 F, and we were already dripping wet with sweat right after the swim. In hindsight, taking the doors off was a bad decision though I was considering the comfort of my team. This was but one lesson I would learn as the leader of a convoy: physical comfort never takes precedence over bodily safety. Could it be that same way between physical comfort and the spiritual safety as well?

We approached a roundabout intersection and realized that we needed to exit half way on the other side to go west toward Baledogal. As we entered the roundabout, we soon saw that all the exits were blocked. The attackers also quickly rolled in an old, broken down bus to block us in further. We had been ambushed by what looked like a mixture of the enemy and locals trying to steal whatever they could, including the fuel tanks. They attacked us from every side. Without doors on the HUMV, my driver and I were sitting ducks. Luckily, because they did not have the means for many weapons, they were using slingshots and clubs, but it became hand-to-hand combat within seconds.

Our rules of engagement at the time of the ambush were "Do not fire unless fired upon first." We had made this very clear to the convoy before leaving. It was only a matter of days before our sector was proclaimed to be an official combat zone, but until then we had to comply with these rules. I was proud that not a shot was let off from our convoy, but we were clearly in danger of losing our lives or becoming prisoners of war.

A man rushed to the side of my vehicle swinging a club at me, and I swung back for my life. Seeing the trouble, my driver started to get out of the vehicle to help me, but I yelled at him to get back in and drive as I put my gun up in my aggressor's face. I yelled as I clicked back the hammer without pulling the trigger, hoping fear would make him step back. It was just enough time for me to radio the HEMMT driver to slam through the bus. He radioed back that he was afraid of damaging the new vehicle. With a few choice words while keeping my eyes on the man in front of me, I ordered him to ram it full stroke to get us out of the mess. He complied in the nick of time, and we got through safely with nothing but a few nicks and bruises, including the vehicles.

Once again, God was with me just like He'd been in Denmark. There was no question that it was grace that saved our little convoy that day. Throughout my time in Somalia, with its disunity, physical discomfort, insecurity and unsafe authority, along with its starvation and combat in the middle of its normal civilian environment made it seemed as if the Lord was showing me what my life without Him; what a world without safe boundaries could look like if I really chose to go that route. This was a look at what unhealthy controlling authority does to people; one I hadn't really experienced or known before. God was giving me a real good look what it meant for people to run from His guidance, like Eve having to live outside of the garden. Healthy boundaries are good; they bring freedom, something the people of Somalia lost when the warlords took control. It was a good metaphor for the outcomes our choices can bring us and what might happen to me if I kept ignoring His healthy, safe guidance and struggling for power.

I came back from Somalia a different person, somewhat more mature in worldly ways, but still not seeing God's finger pointing to His way. Writing this I still get infuriated at my own obstinacy. He was trying to show me, but my blindness had to take me to my own personal Somalia.

At times I think this is like a dancing couple. Jesus is the excellent dancer who is supposed to be the lead, but we keep trying to take the lead, stepping on his feet, awkwardly stumbling. There is an Irish song by Sydney Carter called *The Lord of the Dance*. The chorus goes, "Dance, then, wherever you may be, I am the Lord of the Dance, said He. And I'll lead you all, wherever you may be, and I'll lead you all in the dance, said He." Notice the way the lyrics say, "*I'll* lead you." It doesn't say that we should lead on. Using the metaphor of a dance, it speaks of the hard times Jesus went through in His time on earth and how we need to learn this dance to go through our lives with joy. It is a beautiful reflection of Psalms 87:6-7. "In His register of peoples He writes: 'These are her children, and while they dance they will sing. In You, all find their home.'" (Psalm 87:6-7, from the Grail Psalms Copyright © 1963, The Grail, England) There is a definite feeling of home when we learn the dance and sing while doing it. We can find joy in the hardships instead of embarrassing ourselves by stumbling through our life journey.

I was completely separated from my husband while I was in Somalia. This allowed me to distance myself from him as much as I wanted. Without the reminder that I had promised unity, I was able to distance from the responsibility. Other soldiers told me that Jason had asked their spouses to send word to me asking how I was and to write more. I only wrote one or two letters. I wasn't trying to be mean to him though it was. I was being selfish with my time. I wanted to be alone in the adventure without the world back home. This distance made redeployment even harder.

Yes, I enjoyed the reunion at first, the hugs, the long embrace, and the feeling that I had been missed. But soon it wore off, and reality flooded in and more than ever. I was faced with the routine of needing to give of myself and trying to find unity once again. Arguments erupted because we had learned to live without this unity and my "self" wanted to preserve the independence it had gained. Instead of embracing the strength that unity could provide, and learning that courage is found "in being extraordinary in the ordinary"; as St Therese of Lisieux speaks of, I found myself battling against it, fighting for self-sufficiency and power. But I didn't know that then. Jason also found this hard and battled it in his own way by becoming close to his students and training and spending more time and money on them and on his bicycle training. We both hid from it by keeping busy like we'd always been able to do in college.

In one instance, I sensed his relationship with a young woman was too close, and it caused us farther separation. Though my pride battled against the strength of unity with Jason, I could not understand his trying to find it with others. My "self" envied what it did not want. I wanted to have my cake and to eat it, too, as the saying goes.

Before we redeployed to the states and Ft. Rucker in the early spring 1993, Jason was going to coach another swim camp and invited a small group up to train at the little airbase swimming pool. When I witnessed him being more intimate with one of the young campers than I felt was appropriate, I felt angry and jealous. The next day when we had to take the kids back home, we dropped her off last, and I was sure it was on purpose. He told me to wait for him in the car while he walked her to her door. I was fuming as I watched him give her a hug.

When we got back, I saw a girl's necklace with a Jewish star on it on our bedside table. I knew it had to be hers because she was the only one with a Jewish background. This opened up a huge argument. I accused him of having an inappropriate relationship with this girl, and he denied it, saying the girls probably sat on our bed and talked during the day and left it there. My yelling at him didn't solve a thing, but I was trying to alleviate the hurt. I cooled off, thinking perhaps he was right, but it stayed with me. I wanted the power of blame to linger but at the same time wanted the peace and truth back. We worked it out, but things became strained between us.

We left Europe after three years when I was redeployed to the states for the required Advanced Officer Training course. I had been awarded the rank of captain (CPT) in June, before we left, and it was time to plan out my career more seriously.

In the military, we had an evaluation system for commissioned and non-commissioned officers. The front of the form had areas for write-ups about the officer's performance. The back had an evaluation block system with empty squares on the left to put an X in. Next to each square were little icons in the shape of men. The top block has only one man. This is the top and best evaluation. The next has two men, the next three, the middle has several and then it tapers off again until the bottom block has one lonely guy next to it. Ideally, there was only one officer of each type rated to the single top block, in other words, all platoon leaders or all CW2s were rated together for that specific job, by each superior. So, for example, based on the commander's estimation, only one out of the three to five platoon leaders in a unit received the single "top block" because he or she rose above the rest. The others would receive two or three blocks. Whatever block you received on your evaluation rated you for that rating period (at least one a year, depending on if you changed positions). To advance to colonel, you pretty much have to get either one or two blocks for all your evaluations. It is nearly unheard of to get all single top blocks.

My commanders had written in all of my evaluation how exemplary my integrity was and what a shining example I had been for other young officers. I had all single top blocks the whole seven years I was in the active duty service, save the last one, which I will explain further on. I say this not out of pride but to illustrate how committed to the military I was and how important it had become to me, like a god, while I allowed my marriage to fall apart and my faith to be waylaid like some ambushed convoy. This apple of success wasn't bad in itself. In fact, it is a way of evaluating faithful service, but my performance did not stem from being with God nor giving Him the glory and so was not coupled with discernment or selfless service. The true test of leadership was yet to be fought off the battlefield.

We went back to Ft. Rucker, Al where I graduated again with honors, being the most physically fit soldier in the class. At twenty-eight, I was still able to compete and excel according to the more stringent men's standards because I felt it should be all one. I ran two miles in thirteen minutes, did 110 pushups in two minutes, and 110 sit-ups in two minutes —consecutively.

The requirements were different for men than for women, except for the sit-up standards. Because I could max out the men's standards, I definitely maxed out the women's, thereby making my score even higher than my male counterparts. The men's standard to max the run for a twenty-eight year old was 13:18, but as I got older, my run time was slowing down. It was getting dangerously close to not maxing the men's standards but because the women's was only 15:48, I always maxed the standard. There were men in our unit who would have had a better chance at beating my score if we were graded fairly all on the same standard. I was proud that I could max the men's requirements, but I really didn't want to know if any of the men could actually beat me according to their own standard. Subconsciously I didn't want to see it, so it was advantageous to not care how high my score was over max according to which standard they graded me on. Looking back, I have to say that this was an unfair advantage to women, especially given that we were all doing the same mission, requiring the same physical fitness regardless of sex. It was another way in which pride did not allow me to face the reality of my situation. Plus, I didn't want to give up the advantageous rewards afforded to officers who won this award, such as first selections to aircraft transitions in our Advanced Course, or just the recognition it would give me over the others who were left among the many.

I was still in top shape physically with all top block evaluations, and now I had Air Borne, Air Assault, flight wings, Allied Force experience, deployment, and flight experience in Europe. I also had experience in logistics and being a platoon leader. I had earned many awards and badges, but I still needed this required Advanced Officer Training Course. There was nothing stopping me from a wonderful military career.

After graduating in February 1994 from the Advanced Officer Training Course, top graduates were offered flight transitions to other aircraft to help determine our career paths. The UH-1H Huey I had been rated in was slowly being phased out of the active duty Army units, so it was clear I would have to take a transition to another aircraft. The question was which one. Utility and support missions or attack? My former S3 officer who I had worked under in Europe now worked as a major in Washington DC in officer placement. He phoned me after seeing my advancements and suggested I take up AH-64 attack helicopter transition and go for being the first woman to command an attack unit in the Active Duty Army. He said I would be granted whatever I wanted because of my record. Being young and impressionable with "self" right there in the forefront, I decided to go for it. If I had been in my faith, I would have asked God what was right for me. If I had listened to His warnings in Denmark and Somalia, I would have seen where I was headed, but "self" went strongly and blindly into worldly promises of success and fame.

Though I had been given little reminders that I wasn't all-powerful and self-sufficient, I blindly ignored them. I wanted to believe that I was sought after, important, powerful. I even fully wanted and expected the media to start asking me for interviews. I had heard that the four other women who had gotten the transition before me had been given such treatment, and they weren't even in leadership roles in active duty. It was alluring. The self wanted to shine without realizing that it wasn't ready for such responsibility.

Like always, I was deciding autonomously what was good for my career. The promise of success and fame blocked out any subconscious warnings or even other options that were fully available to me, like the better option of taking a company command in a support mission career field through a UH60 transition. The UH60 was an excellent aircraft and a mission that would have been much more in line with my training. It even included repelling and troop transport missions, which I loved. But like the Barbara Streisand song *Lesson to Be Learned*, I chose "my" right way and later wondered, "why the road I chose would take the wrong turn; why my heart would break and get burned."

I requested the AH-64 transition, received the slot, and started the training a few weeks after graduation right there at Ft. Rucker. I had only been in support roles up until then, and had really loved it. Why didn't I think this was good enough? It was more than good enough, but I was greedy, reaching out for a great looking apple I was not ready for. I had flown dignitaries and generals around Europe but had not been trained in tactics. I knew nothing about threat identification of enemy tanks and targets, calling in artillery, or the fluid front-line battle. But the role I was entering into would expect me to be an expert and make decisions for my unit based on past experience that I did not have.

My desire to be in the limelight and be the best I could be overshadowed the fact that I was not ready for what I had committed to. Somehow I thought that like all other things in my life that I could "will" it to be learned. I would just work harder and throw myself into the necessary training to get up to speed. I went in with two strikes against me: lack of experience and being the first female ever to be in this role.

The power struggles I would experience in my new training and unit came not so much from being female, though this was surely a large part of it since they had never been led by a woman, but more from the fact that I was now a captain entering into a higher leadership role without experience. It was downright dangerous for all involved. Lieutenants coming out of flight school are expected to learn as they go, but captains going into a command should be much further along. Both the new instructors and unit knew it, and so did I.

Leaving all of this left unsaid was like a cooking cauldron. It was left unsaid because of my pride and power struggle to be the best, others wanting to say they'd been a part of a new army change, and still others being afraid that they'd be labeled as "prejudiced against females" if they took a stand against it. I felt as if I was expected somehow to simply absorb all this experience and just come out being a great, experienced attack commander despite only having had a few weeks of transition training, and if I didn't, there'd be silent hell to pay. That wasn't the reality though. No, the reality was that I was forcing my way into something I wasn't ready for. And the others shouldn't have been expected to accept me as their new inexperienced leader. This caused animosity from the very people I would need to help me succeed. There is a weakness in pride.

I found myself floundering even in the transition phase while trying to learn the Apache helicopter with its sophisticated armament and night vision systems. Some of the instructors, especially the gunnery instructor pilot, did not like the idea that I was going through the training. He was sarcastic and rude while flying, showing me the bare minimum, leaving me to tackle the nuances of highly technical gunnery on my own. This made for a very stressful environment in the cockpit.

I remember one time when we stopped to refuel, I got out of the aircraft and unplugged from the intercom system. Normally, you can keep your helmet plugged into the communication wire because it's long enough if you are just outside the aircraft door during refueling, especially if you are with an instructor pilot that may want to use the down time to explain and critique the flight training you just received. But I unplugged because we were almost yelling at each other as we argued. I needed to be silent and regroup without his anger and stress.

The refueler was astonished to see a captain and warrant officer going at it like we were and was uncertain how to address us. I remember looking at him in an apologetic way for the way we had behaved. My drive and ambition, though, would not allow me to be defeated. I kept on trying because I didn't know the word for fail or possibly couldn't or wouldn't see truth. This only infuriated the instructor more. The worst part of it was that the instructor had personal ties to the instructor pilots at my new assignment and was paving the way with his comments to them with every turn. I knew this but could do nothing but try harder to change his opinion of me, which did not happen. It only made things worse. I began to see that this was one challenge I wasn't going to overcome by sheer determination and hard work, though I tried and tried to do so.

Finally, I graduated from the Apache transition on July 7, 1994, and headed out for my new assignment in the United States Air Calvary. I knew I was heading off to a unit that, for the most part, did not want women and had been prepped by my Ft. Rucker Transition gunnery instructor's degrading comments. This was the start of my personal Somalia.

CHAPTER 2

Running from the Burning Truth

When I arrived at my new unit, I checked into the officer's hotel, which also served as a receiving station for newly arriving officer soldiers and families to be stationed there. Jason had gotten there early so he could pick out some land in a subdivision where we were going to build a home. He had made all the arrangements and decisions, and the house was nearly done.

The S3 (operations officer) of the new unit, a major, came the second day after I arrived and knocked on our door. He was a big Jewish man, about six-foot-five and full of life. I liked him. He gave me a chance right from the start. He told me to get my things together because he was taking me out to the field to prepare and do reconnaissance for gunnery. He expected me to write the operations order for our deployment and execution of the unit's gunnery mission coming up in a month. So I got ready and left Jason wondering when I'd return and what to do in the meantime. My stomach sank when I thought of what I had gotten myself into. I was uncertain about so many things — the future, my knowledge base, how the unit would receive me — and now I was doing a reconnaissance of a flight helicopter gunnery I had never done, for an attack operations order I had to write with no idea where to start.

I was introduced to the unit and its new technologies so quickly that it left my head swimming. To my new commander's credit he decided to leave me in the S3 (Operations and Planning Center) for about four months before allowing me to take over command of A Troop so I could become accustomed to the attack role and learn for a time. I felt like a yellow neon sign for all soldiers to gawk at and silently criticize. Everything I did was magnified, which made it very hard to learn without the mercy of learning from mistakes. The IPs (instructor pilots) had already been prepped by the Ft. Rucker pilot as to what to expect and were expecting the worst. It was as if I had already failed before arriving. The stress was incredible, and there were no other women I could converse with, no one who could understand me. I was on my own. After all, wasn't that what I always wanted, independence? Only now it looked a lot scarier than before. I kept asking myself if I'd gotten in over my head.

"Every one to whom much is given, of him will much be required; and of him to whom men commit much they will demand the more." (Luke 12:48 RSVCE). When I said yes to the responsibility of taking on the AH64 captain command slot, I said yes to all that meant, but I had never really counted the cost. "For which of you, desiring to build a tower, does not first sit down and count the cost, whether he has enough to complete it? Otherwise, when he has laid a foundation, and is not able to finish, all who see it begin to mock him, saying, 'This man began to build, and was not able to finish'" (Luke 14:28-30 RSVCE). In this verse, Jesus was telling the disciples that they had to give of themselves totally for the mission and to rely on His strength, not their own. When I accepted the role of commander, I did not seek out God's strength through prayer, I was not considering the good of the whole, the betterment of the unit, or the army, just myself. Therefore, I should not have been surprised to find myself alone, misunderstood, frustrated, and ill equipped.

The lack of morality in the unit was something I was not ready for either. Though I had not been in my faith, I had been in a supportive flying unit that had women. To some extent it maintained a moral decency that this one lacked. Soldiers fooled around on their wives with other wives. There were constant sexual innuendos and little cuts here and there. The pilots walked around like cocks in a hen house. I felt like the warlords of Somalia were breathing down my neck, taunting me to sink or swim.

Jason became assistant coach of the post's high school swim team, which was a volunteer position Jason did out of his passion. He also started to scout out new bike routes and got into rock climbing so that he would stay fit. The cost of his cycling and athletic ventures was in the thousands at times and was becoming a financial drain. Our yearly CPT and flight pay was about $34,000 at the time. This was nice but not a budget that could handle a lot of spending. One time, he spent our entire paycheck for the month on rock climbing equipment. We didn't have anything left to live on for the rest of the month. I went off on him, telling him to take it back and get the money we would need. Even Jason did not understand the stress I was under. But neither did I seek to understand his stress. He was coping with his new surroundings as best as he knew how. When I told Jason that he needed to get a job to pay for his new hobby, he applied and was hired in the local army post exchange. But he didn't last long there before he was let go for the allegation of stealing from the till, which was not investigated or proved. And so our lives went on downhill. We talked of this allegation but let it hang in the air like a lead balloon.

The old feelings I had just before leaving for Somalia were coming back. I wanted to be secure and have Jason work and me stay at home taking care of children. I longed for this in the depths of my soul. I wanted a relief from the burden I had taken on and I wanted our lives to be wholesome. Jason and I discussed adoption. We had never used contraception because we had never had gotten pregnant. I thought I was infertile because I had temporary paralysis from the waist down from scarlet fever I had as a child. Jason thought perhaps he was impotent from all of the intense physical exercise he did. In any case, it didn't seem as if we could have children. We were not enjoying intimacy much at this point either so pregnancy was even harder to achieve. Nor was it really something that fit into the attack pilot and commander role I now had pursued. Overlooking our own relationship failures and distance from our faith, we tried to seek some type of fulfillment and normalcy by starting a family. We were seeking the answers to these desires in a child.

Jason was quite proactive in the adoption process, and soon we were connected with a family whose grandchild had gotten pregnant at an early age and couldn't care for her child. The baby was only about a month old. Jason actually got to go and hold the baby — how close we came to adoption. But at the last minute, the grandmother just couldn't see her flesh and blood be separated forever from her and decided to raise the child herself. She was a giving person and was not trying to gain the child for selfish reasons. It was as if our Lord was trying to show us what we could have if we but turned away from selfishness.

To be in union with Jesus is to give of self and die to self again and again. I was not in union with our Lord nor His church. I was living in and for myself. He tried to show this to me so gently in many ways, but my hardheartedness would not allow me to hear or see His truths. The more I battled this in my life, though I started to see how it was harming me, the more frustrated and burdensome my life became. He kept calling me but I would not come. "Come to Me, all you that are weary and are carrying heavy burdens, and I will give you rest. Take My yoke upon you and learn from Me, for I am gentle and humble in heart, and you will find rest for your souls. For My yoke is easy, and My burden is light" (Matthew 11:28-30 NRSV). If we decide to die to self and live in and for Christ, then our burdens are not heavy as if we were all alone. My burdens became much, much heavier as I continued to go down this rebellious path.

Our relationship became worse daily. We were no longer intimate with each other, neither in marital relations nor in our conversations. Everything was surface talk about food, what to do, where to go, the swim team, how training went, or work, but nothing of depth. Again, it was a perfect reflection of our faith.

I remember once we took a rare walk together in the suburbs around our home just outside of the base. We were walking near an area of row houses when we saw a couple outside on their front yard, arguing and yelling angrily. The man got aggressive and hit the woman — hard — then continued to punch her around the face as she tried to get free.

Other people just walked and stared. It was incredible to me that no one was doing or saying anything. I started to go over to them, but Jason grabbed my arm gently and said, "Stay out of it, Marie. It's not our concern. We don't want to get involved. It will only be trouble. I don't know that I could fight him off if he turned on us." I argued with him, saying that at least I wanted to yell that we'd call the police. My starting to go over to them must have struck a chord in the man because he stopped hitting her, and they went inside. We never did call the police. I still feel badly about my inactivity, our indecision, our doing nothing.

That's how I felt Jason was in life. He just wanted things to go smoothly, to ignore the truth and what was really going on. I, on the other hand, wanted to rush in without thinking about what would happen in the aftermath or who it would affect.

It seemed to me that I was seeing power struggles everywhere in life, between pilots vying for PIC status, males and females, husbands and wives, and between pride and humility. It was raging inside of me and even silently in my own marriage as our differences grew into a larger and larger gap. The memory of that couple stayed with me and for good reason.

A boy from Jason's swim team in Europe called saying his parents were going through a divorce. He was eighteen and looking to escape. He planned to find a job and then go on to college. He asked if he could come live with us. Wanting to help out in some small way, we said sure, but it was mainly a diversion to fill our emptiness.

This boy arrived and neither he nor Jason were able to find work. I would come home to find them watching TV with dishes piled in the sink. I felt more like a visitor than being in my own home. I became more and more frustrated with the situation. I started to stay later at work, coming home only to plug into earphones to shut them out and escape. Jason and I were totally disconnected with one another as man and wife. We became more like acquaintances who lived with each other because of some obligation. Soon this boy went off to college, but his absence made the distance in our marriage seem even bigger. Now there was no one else to lay blame on, just the two of us.

About four months after we moved there, and right after our unit deployed back from gunnery, I took over command of one of the troops in the Cavalry on October 4, 1994. I was in charge of ten aircraft, including AH64 Apache and OH58D helicopters, trucks, and thirty-three officers and enlisted personnel to operate and maintain them all. Being the first woman in the U.S. Army to take command of an active duty attack unit, I was in the papers and on the news. Pride grew without giving the glory to God or asking if it was what He wanted. I took the credit along with the burden that God knew was much too heavy for my shoulders to handle. All the while I was feeling empty, alone. I was missing the support role of the UH-1 but couldn't allow myself to realize that truth. I needed to see the truth and my own inability and weakness without it, but I continually ran from it as if it were a burning light that would wound me.

Before our deployment to gunnery and me taking over command, I met Cruz, a CW2 who was the maintenance pilot for the troop I'd be taking over. He came into the S3 operations office where I was working to introduce himself. Unlike the other pilots, he was nice to me. It gave me hope that I may fit in eventually.

Not long after our redeployment back from our gunnery mission and after my change of command, my unit received orders for another deployment. This deployment happened on the 21st of October, only seventeen days after I had taken command, two months after gunnery and only three-and-a-half months since I'd graduated from the Apache Transition. Jason didn't see me most of that first year.

We were performing drug interdiction along the Mexican border out of an Army base at Ft. Huachuca, Arizona, so off we went. Again, I was happy for the distraction from the mess of my personal life. I hoped that maybe the time away would fix what I didn't know how to fix. This mission would take us away for approximately a month or more and we would be hours away along the Mexican border. We flew out in formation loaded up for an exciting adventure.

This being my first action as a commander, I truly wanted to shine in this mission. I also wanted to get in a lot of flight time to perfect my flight performance and get to know the men and the aircraft that belonged to my command. I bunked in the same barracks as my troop but had my own room.

At first, our troop aircraft maintenance was poor, so I made it my goal to make it the best in the squadron. This would make us, rather me, look good, and I would get in more flight time. Besides, maintenance was something I was familiar with. I could cling to it to improve my feeling of belonging and standing. I spent countless hours on the tarmac looking over logbooks and getting up to speed on maintenance. We had daily meetings with the colonel on the status of our aircraft and what we were doing about it. I knew every question and was prepared with a proactive answer. If I couldn't fit in with the pilots by being popular, I would fit in by being the best where I could, regardless of what they thought. I didn't see that this was mostly for me and not for the unit. I didn't recognize that leaders are held to a higher standard of giving than others.

We got our missions in and flew as many hours as we could. After we got back to the base from patrolling the border, we would tick off in chalk on the side of the AH64 how many pounds of drugs our particular aircraft had intercepted. It became a kind of trophy. Then after each mission, I checked the aircraft readiness so I could stay on top of our maintenance. I should have challenged Cruz; the maintenance pilot and officer, to do this and report to me, thus giving him a chance to shine more and allowing me to spend more time with the other men in our unit, spreading myself out for the whole, not just for what made me look good in the moment.

The more I spent time on maintenance, the more time I spent with the maintenance pilot. I even would take the run ups; running up the aircraft on the tarmac after a maintenance repair going over temperatures, checking for a normal flight operation, so I could get more experience. Cruz also happened to be the top gun from our recent gunnery deployment and was a good pilot. He had a charming personality that drew everyone to him. His heart seemed genuine. He stood six feet with a muscular, manly build, not overweight and not underweight. He had dark wavy hair, blue eyes, and an irresistibly mischievous boy's smile. He was four years older than me and loved the 70s along with heavy rock music and his '76 SS Chevy Camaro. Whereas the other pilots didn't always seem to take their positions seriously, he really cared about the Army and absolutely loved being a pilot. He was a soldier's soldier, one a commander could lean on and trust.

Maintenance guys seemed to be the unheard of, unsung heroes in aviation. But I respected his knowledge and his interest in his job, something other commanders had not done. In return, he respected and appreciated me, as well. Feeling appreciated in that unit was rare for me and possibly for him. Perhaps that's why we felt close.

After a long time of putting our noses to the grindstone, the colonel financed a mini day trip to the historic town of Tombstone. I decided to stay behind to further understand maintenance and the soldiers working on the runway. I should have gone with the big group and gotten to know the others. I had lunch with the small group of maintenance pilots, and though we talked about maintenance, we shared about our lives, too. As we got to know each other better, we felt more comfortable. I discovered that Cruz was also having a similar kind of marital problem (selfishness) only he had three kids. He really loved his kids, but the marriage seemed to be going nowhere, and he seemed to be lost in it.

On our unit's redeployment trip back home, we stopped at an airfield to refuel. I was flying with my troop's (IP) Instructor Pilot. Getting back in our aircraft, I noticed an odor that smelled like an electrical fire upon start up. Because the air goes through the vents of the Apache in the front cockpit first, I picked it up before my instructor pilot who was sitting in the back seat. I mentioned this to him and said we had better check it out before taking off. We were supposed to fly back in formation and didn't have any time to spare, making my back seat pilot anxious to get going. He said, "I don't smell anything. Let's get going." I insisted that we get out and check.

Using a frustrated and disrespectful tone, he said he'd get out and check while I stayed hooked in. When he opened the back engine coiling, a flash of fire burst out at him. He ran up to me, yelling, "Get out, get out, it's on fire!" I rushed to get out quickly as we radioed for the fire truck to put out the fire. With a whole load of fuel on board it could have been devastating, not only to the $8 million dollar aircraft but to us, as well. Fires are more common on helicopters than one might think, and the fuel we used, Jet Propellant 8 (JP8), is a kerosene-based jet fuel similar to civilian Jet A fuel with a flash point of one hundred degrees Fahrenheit. Though it has a high flash point, it can be ignited rapidly if a flame is present. It is dangerous and burns hot enough in a running aircraft to melt skin. I've seen pilots who have suffered such burns all over their bodies; there is little time for escape.

Because the rest of the unit was taking off for home, we had to call back our maintenance pilot, Cruz to have him test fly the aircraft after switching out the burned up standby generator that had caused the fire. The repair and test flying took all afternoon, requiring us to fly back the next day. Since we didn't need both the aircraft that the maintenance test pilot flew and ours, I sent my IP back in the aircraft Cruz had flown along with his other pilot. As commander, I should have gone back to watch over the redeployment process, but I didn't want to return back to my life any sooner than necessary. And this allowed time for the maintenance pilot and me to spend quality time together again.

When we finally got back the next day on November 18, Cruz's wife and family were waiting for him, as was my husband Jason. I remember feeling in the pit of my stomach how wrong it all felt, how I didn't want it to be real any longer. But I smiled and hugged Jason, saying I was glad to be back and ready to unpack to spend some off time for a day or two before getting back to work, though that wasn't really what I felt. I wanted to go back, to be talking with Cruz, to be away from this emptiness I felt when I was around my own husband, an emptiness I helped create but didn't want to solve.

Jason and I decided to take a break during the Christmas holiday and go hiking in the mountains of Texas bordering the Rio Grande and Mexico. We went for a whole two weeks, hiking and sleeping out in the wilderness, but it was strained. At one point, I began singing Christmas carols along a trail, and he became annoyed with me, I think for reminding him of the wholesome family Christmas we were missing. I didn't see that, wasn't aware of what I or we missed. I sensed it somehow but hadn't connected it with the songs. He didn't want to be in any photos, allowing for maybe one shot on the way out of the national park.

With full packs, the hiking was hard and became tiresome, even though we were surrounded by beauty. We even got to sit with some local people in a natural hot spring that borders the Rio Grande. None of this pulled us together, though it should have. It only caused us to pull farther away from each other.

Soon after we came back from the Texas hike, Jason left for a thirty-day mountain hike in Mexico with one of the pilots from my unit. The hike required oxygen because the mountains were so high. Jason was looking for something to prove himself, something to define him. While he was gone, I threw myself into even more maintenance and our unit's mission.

Cruz was also having increasing trouble in his marriage at this time, so we started to spend more time together at work. Soon rumors were flying around that we were having an affair. One day, one of my lieutenants, the Apache platoon leader, came up to Cruz, another crew chief, and me down in the hanger and started to make small talk, telling us about an affair between a troop leader in our unit and an enlisted soldier, that had been investigated about a year ago. He had seen photos of the two together that someone had taken so that they could be accused. I remember thinking it was odd that he brought up such a topic to us and filed it back of my mind.

Fraternization in the military, as one might expect, has been known to compromise the unit's productivity and morale. It is subject to military justice. The Uniform Code of Military Justice (UCMJ) is a congressional code of military criminal law applicable to all military members. It basically tells a soldier what he can and cannot do. If a soldier goes against anything in this code, he will be liable to investigation, trial, loss of rank, removal from service, and even jail time. UCMJ article 134 and its subparagraphs along with AR600-20 paragraphs 4-14 (Army Regulation subject to ruling of UCMJ) state that relationships between soldiers of different rank are prohibited if they:

1. Compromise, or appear to compromise, the integrity of supervisory authority or the chain of command.
2. Cause actual or perceived partiality or unfairness.
3. Involve, or appear to involve, the improper use of rank or position for personal gain.
4. Are, or are perceived to be, exploitative or coercive in nature.

5. Create an actual or clearly predictable adverse impact on discipline, authority, morale, or the ability of the command to accomplish its mission.

Due to the ruling of UCMJ and the story my platoon leader was telling me, you can imagine why it should have struck a chord with me. It was as if God was giving me a chance, helping me to see truth, to see where I was going — only I didn't see it. I hadn't seen my relationship at that point as at all compromising my professionalism or the unit's, in fact, I thought otherwise. I simply didn't see the handwriting on the wall and ran from the prompting to truth.

Not long after, the colonel came to talk to me in my office one day because my Apache lieutenant, the one who told us the story, had reported the allegation to him that Cruz and I may be having an affair. I told my commander that nothing was going on, but that I was spending a lot of time with maintenance trying to get my feet on the ground. "Isn't it showing in our performance?" I asked, and, "Hasn't our maintenance up time become the best in the squadron?" He agreed and left.

With all that, I hadn't realized that indeed our relationship was becoming inappropriate, especially, if others perceived that we were spending too much time with each other. I should have taken the second hint given to me when the colonel came to talk with me seriously, but instead I brushed it off as foolish immaturity on their part.

I went home and discussed the whole thing with Jason so that he was aware of the allegations. I even remember asking him if he thought my involvement was inappropriate. He told me that as long as we weren't physical, and it wasn't real, he didn't see any problem with how I was acting. Subconsciously, I wanted him to say yes, to fight for us, but his approval only led me to believe it was all ok and innocent. My selfishness and desire to believe what I wanted was creating a burden that would soon become too big to sustain.

During this time, one of my crew chiefs, who was married, was having an affair with another soldier's wife, and it was my job to address the problem. I called him into my office and told him he had to quit seeing this woman. I told him that I would write it into his record but that we would give him a chance to end the affair without further investigation. We had a good meeting, and he left without any further damage to his career. Through this, God was giving me my own third chance before my relationship with Cruz became harmful to both of us. God knew this temptation would prove too much for me if I kept going on the path I was taking.

Many times in my life God has had to give me three or more chances in different ways and through different people to hear His guidance in a matter before I actually listened. If I had listened, I would have found safety, refuge from the storm brewing up. "Every word of God proves true; He is a shield to those who take refuge in Him" (Proverbs, 30:5). Subconsciously, I was wrestling with God, playing with fire. Like the standby generator on fire in the aircraft that day, I should have gotten out as soon as possible when I smelled the problem . . . I should have listened to others pointing out the danger.

"So if you think you are standing, watch out that you do not fall. No testing has overtaken you that is not common to everyone. God is faithful, and He will not let you be tested beyond your strength, but with the testing, He will also provide the way out so that you may be able to endure it" (1 Corinthians 10:12-13 NRSV) But once again because of my hardheartedness and veiled perception I didn't take the way out He was showing me.

Jason decided to go to Wisconsin for a bike race over my twenty-ninth birthday. I felt disrespected by him for leaving me during my birthday. Being so into myself and not seeing he was also searching for answers, I blamed him for not loving or caring for me. When Cruz found out it was my birthday, he took me out for a drink at a place that had dancing. In my mind, where Jason had failed, this man had once again filled the emptiness. He asked me for a dance, and the physical closeness made us both aware of what we were flirting with the first time. By the end of the night, we had held hands, and the physical affair had begun.

We talked about it during maintenance test flights together, after work, or over lunch. I think my commander was worried about our involvement being too close though he believed what I had told him. There was a Multiservice Training Operation going on in New

Mexico called Roving Sands 1995. To his credit, the colonel sent me out there to get training and possibly put some distance between Cruz and me.

While I was there, I took a weekend off to visit a cousin of mine who lived out there. It was good for me to talk with her about what was going on as she had been in the military and could understand a bit where I was coming from. I confided in her that my marriage was in trouble, that I was having feelings for another man, that I'd lost respect for my husband, and that I was seriously thinking of leaving him. I didn't talk to her about how the military may see our relationship at that point because I still wasn't fully aware that it was an inappropriate relationship for the unit. She listened and tried to give me some good advice. She shared with me how her own marriage also had problems in the beginning, but they had worked it out, and now were still happily married seven years later. Here was my fourth chance to take what I was doing seriously.

While I was there I received letters from Cruz but not a single one from Jason. Somewhere deep inside I was looking for one, hoping it might come still. What a change from Somalia when I couldn't care less about getting or sending a card to Jason.

After I returned home from the training, I had an overwhelming desire to reach out to Jason to slow down the train of events. I wanted him to fight for us, but he was preparing to leave the next day to take his swim team hiking to the place we'd gone the Christmas before.

Our old friend Ann from our college swim and bike racing teams had moved down near our base and was working only about one hour away. She came to help Jason chaperone. I sat with her in the car in tears telling her that I was thinking about divorce. I told her that I needed Jason to stay and that I wanted him to help me fight temptations. That morning I tried asked Jason to stay home for at least the first day, perhaps because I knew I would be tempted to go on a trip with Cruz while he was gone, and it would be all over. Jason didn't know what I was contemplating, and I couldn't tell him. I wasn't even one hundred percent sure I would go through with it. Jason was too far along in the trip to postpone it, and he was the one in charge. He told me I'd have to wait until he got back to talk it through. That would be too late. It was the last thread of hope for our marriage, and I knew it. I was looking for help, though I know it was selfish in its timing.

After he left with the group and our friend Ann, I cried about the past I'd lost with him and how my own temptations, confusion and desires were taking me into the unknown. But the tears weren't for anyone else but me. They were self-centered, perhaps even accusatory toward Jason. This just seemed to fuel my fire to dust myself off and let it all go. During the time Jason was gone, I spent most of my time at work doing maintenance and being around Cruz.

Cruz and I talked it through and decided to formally go through with our relationship by making a secret plan. We told our spouses that we were going off on a training mission and booked a hotel near the gulf. We had not made love at this point and had only kissed once, but we were no longer looking at the apple. We had picked it off the tree, held it in our hands, and raised it to our lips. "You have heard that it was said, 'You shall not commit adultery.' But I say to you that everyone who looks at a woman lustfully has already committed adultery with her in his heart" (Matthew 5:27-28 RSVCE). After we slept together at the hotel, the affair was in full swing.

When we got back, we thought we were in love, but knew that we had to keep the whole thing a secret or it might destroy our careers. This newness of perceived love left me feeling like the old was no longer pulling me down. I felt young and alive again, whereas before, the only thing I looked forward to was work. The tempter "is a liar and the father of lies" (John 8:44 NRSV). He gives us false hopes, and ruined futures. If we believe in him and his lies, we become his children.

To be considered for the attack role in the Apache transition, we had to take a personality test. The army looked for strong, type A personalities for the attack slots, especially the Apache. Type A women are like Martha (Lk10:38-42): unable to relax, highly competitive, ambitious, high achieving, multi-taskers, and workaholics. Type As are also frustrated by B types. I tested as a strong type A personality as did Cruz. Jason was more a B personality, relaxed and easy going with no real sense of urgency. This new relationship with another type A was exciting for me, on the edge, daring like my personality.

I cared about Jason, but somehow I had started to see him as almost a brother. We hadn't made love in months, we barely saw each other in the house, and when we did, we really didn't seem to have a connection. I just wanted to move out and be on my own without Jason being angry or hurt. I wanted our marriage to fade away like he had in my mind and heart. It was as if Cruz had relit the fire of living in me that had almost been put out. Also, considering the lack of acceptance I had felt from the unit, I felt as if I belonged with Cruz. Another attack pilot, the top gun of the unit, saw me as desirable.

It was April of 1995 and our unit had received orders to draw down and disband, so we didn't think our involvement would hurt the unit if we remained silent. At one point, Cruz suggested that we tell the commander about our affair. He thought we should tell him we were both divorcing our spouses and ask him what we should do about it. I didn't want to though because I didn't think the commander would believe that I'd told him the truth in the first place. The inactivation ceremony for our unit was already coming up on May 17, 1995. I figured that since we were so close to the unit drawing down, it wouldn't matter. So we both kept silent. Cruz's advice to come clean was like a fifth chance, but again I stubbornly ignored the warnings.

After I got back from the Gulf with Cruz, everything had changed. We had decided to move into a hotel on post together for a few days and figure it out. We had started to look for apartments.

When I was home with Jason, I couldn't pretend any longer that things were ok. I didn't want to live with him anymore because it felt as if I were cheating on Cruz. I took a walk in back of our home and tried to think it all through. I remember writing both of their names on the dirt road, just trying to get a clear answer. It was springtime, near Easter. When Jason came back, I told him I wanted a divorce and that I was having the affair. I told him he could stay in the house while we tried to rent it out and that I would move out. I told him he could have anything we owned, including the car. I wouldn't try to take a thing.

He was hurt, of course, but not loud or angry. He asked me to meet him a few times for lunch, which I did regretfully, as if I was appeasing him. I felt it was wasting my time. I was like the rich man feasting on great pleasures in Luke 16 who was indifferent to Lazarus, the poor, starving leper outside his door. The rich man didn't go to Hades just because he didn't help Lazarus but rather for his indifference toward his suffering. I was indifferent to Jason's suffering and indifferent to my sin.

Jason was always nice to me when we met. It was as if we were friends having a small quarrel, almost as if the whole thing wasn't really real. I didn't think through the long-range consequences. I just figured that Jason would always be my friend and be in my life somehow in spite of what I was doing. I now see just how much self was at the center of my life instead of God, real love, His people and His shining truth. Jason tried to get us into counseling, but I refused, thinking that counseling was for weak of mind and for someone who actually thought it could still work. "But He said to me, 'My grace is sufficient for you, for My power is made perfect in weakness'" (2 Corinthians, 12:9 RSVCE). But I didn't want to see God's truth about my own weaknesses, so Jason went by himself. I had made up my mind and taken the leap. By becoming physically intimate with Cruz, I had given myself to him. I was not going back to what I knew. In this, Jason was not the only one I was turning from.

With the unit drawing down, we all had to put in for new assignments. Cruz suggested that we both put in for Korea so that we might end up stationed near each other. Civilian spouses did not normally accompany soldiers there. It was a rough assignment and not a popular place to be stationed. So when I was called up to the brigade commander's office to determine my next move, I told him that I wanted a command in Korea because I knew they couldn't easily fill those slots, and I thought it would ensure me an opportunity to grow as a commander. He was impressed with my dedication to the military and applauded my efforts. As captains, we were only required to lead one company or troop command, not more, so this made an impact on him. Now I feel horrible about misleading that good commander in such a way. May God forgive me.

Not long after we'd started the physical part of our affair, and just after the inactivation ceremony, I found out I was pregnant; something I thought would never happen to me. I had such mixed emotions. On the one hand, I was excited about having a child. On the other hand, I was in the middle of divorcing and possibly remarrying. Not exactly how I'd always dreamt it would be. Now things were serious. Since I couldn't fly in the army and be pregnant, this meant I'd be grounded for sure. But the baby didn't get me down. The thought of being a mother excited me. It never occurred to me to not keep the baby. Though I had done many other things badly, I knew of the value of this life that was part of me. Cruz didn't question keeping the baby either.

The first thing we did was to find an apartment in the next town. It was a small, one bedroom apartment but nice. It was as if we were in a dream, not living realistically somehow. We filed for the divorces with the same attorney at the same time, as if it was something perfectly normal to do. We went on with our lives like a newly dating couple as we waited for the divorces to be final.

Now things were too far along to keep it to myself any longer. I had to tell my parents and my family what was happening. I called my mom and told her the whole thing. I wasn't proud of how it all came about, but I was excited about the baby. My mom took it all in. She wasn't happy with my decisions, but she knew I had made up my mind. I give her so much credit for loving me even though she could not rejoice over my decisions. She listened when I told her how lonely I'd been, how Jason never touched me, held me, or wanted any show of physical affection and how Cruz had slowly filled that emptiness.

My mom didn't turn me away, but my dad took it harder. He remained silent and never spoke to me about it. Things changed between my father and me after that day for a long, long time.

My sister and her husband sent letters to us, trying to help us out in their own way, but none of them tried to convince me that what I was doing was wrong. They were all too nice. I needed some straightforward truth from them, a kick in the pants with love, so to speak. Some call it tough love, but none of them could do it or thought it was their place. They all felt badly for Jason. After all, he was part of our family, too.

Even Jason's mom called me wanting to hear from me why I was asking for a divorce, wondering if Jason had done anything wrong. She was sure it was all Jason's doing and wanted me to explain. I tried to tell her the best way I could why I had chosen the path I took without telling her everything about the affair. I tried to be nice but mostly honest. I think she wanted to make some sense of it all, to really understand what was going on. But nothing made me feel badly enough to stop what I was doing.

The apartment time was almost surreal. We acted as if everything was happy, new, and ok, though I knew it wasn't. We did normal things a new couple does like laundry and cooking. We even had his three children over to meet me. We bought expensive new furniture. This was the first time I had ever bought furniture on credit. I wasn't used to doing that, but we got credit easily and bought the really nice stuff. I remember Cruz saying, "It's about time we live for ourselves." Somehow I thought he was right, like our spouses had been mooching off us. It was as if Amos, speaking about the Israelites and their complacent self indulgence, was watching us too and saying, "'Woe to those who are at ease in Zion, and to those who feel secure on the mountain of Samaria, the notable men of the first of the nations, to whom the house of Israel come! Woe to those who lie upon beds of ivory, and stretch themselves upon their couches...but are not grieved over the ruin of Joseph! Therefore they shall now be the first of those to go into exile, and the revelry of those who stretch themselves shall pass away. The Lord GOD has sworn by himself' (says the LORD, the God of hosts): 'I abhor the pride of Jacob, and hate his strongholds; and I will deliver up the city and all that is in it.'" (Amos 6:1, 4, 6, 7-8 RSVCE). We didn't realize it then, but we too would enter into our own personal exile.

I received another warning, a sense of truth trying to get in, when we had our first argument. It was over laundry. He'd never done it in his marriage, and we just did it as we needed to ourselves in my home. He was hard and controlling, acting as if it was beneath him, like it was woman's work. I didn't like it, and it scared me. I asked myself, "Could I have been wrong about him after all this?" Somehow it was ok to be complacent and self-indulgent with other people, but it was altogether different when we did it to each other. He left the apartment acting self-righteous, and I went to do the laundry. I felt the weight of the whole thing on my shoulders. I wanted this to be a team thing, not lopsided like it had been with Jason.

I filled the bath, got in it to soak, and just cried and cried. I cried about the uncertainty of this "perceived" certainty I thought I finally had. The whole mess finally seemed real to me in that moment. I said to myself, "I'm too far into this to back out now. This isn't real. It'll pass." So I stuffed it deep, deep down and told myself it was nothing, that we'd talk it through, and that he hadn't really meant it.

Soon the same lieutenant who had suspected us from the beginning and who had talked with us about the pictures of the other troop leader's affair wanted to prove he had been right all along. He followed us back to our apartment without us knowing, hid behind some bushes, and watched to see if we went into the apartment together. He then went back and reported all to the commander. Someone called and questioned the apartment complex office to see if we'd both signed the lease together there so they could prove that there was an inappropriate relationship between us. They gave them all the information they needed for the colonel to call me into his office.

Going into the commander's office that day was humbling. Even though the unit was officially inactivated by this time, we still had a skeleton group left to finish up handing in equipment and out-processing soldiers to their new units, so our headquarters was still organized in their offices. Our squadron commander's office was located near the headquarter offices and the S1 section (the army's human resources). When I walked through the office, I had to pass the enlisted soldiers who worked there. They knew what was going on. It was silent, but I could feel the looks burning into my back. The colonel was so angry that he didn't even look at me as I walked in. He was furious that I had misled him.

I had no recourse, nothing to defend myself with. I just stood at attention pregnant, silently defeated and listened to him say my career in the army had come to an end because of my bad decisions. I didn't try to explain or negate anything, but he didn't give me time to explain either. He told me he was giving me a chance to get out of the military on a general discharge under honorable conditions. Either that or he would launch an official investigation, which could even mean jail time. After all those top blocks, here came my new evaluation block . . . bottom of the heap.

I hadn't told anyone about the pregnancy. Army Aviation did ground pilots from flight until after the birth of a baby, but I wasn't flying at the time because the unit had drawn down — not because I had told anyone

I was pregnant. I was biding my time. The battle dress uniform (BDU) hid my growing womb well so that it was possible.

In a way, I was partly relieved to finally be out from under the pressure of the attack army environment, but I had loved my career, the army, the soldiers, working hard, the challenges. I loved the activity, and my pride loved the status and the looks I got walking around in a flight suit. I knew all this would change drastically and very soon. My soul was silent within me, almost empty. I didn't know what to feel or what would happen.

"Pride goes before destruction and a haughty spirit before a fall. It is better to be of a lowly spirit with the poor than to divide the spoils with the proud" (Proverbs 16:18-19 RSVCE). Well, here I was reaping the "spoils," but it wasn't at all what I thought it would be. It wasn't freedom or newness of life. It felt empty and cold. I had always been in control of situations in the military and allowed to decide the course of my career, but now there was nothing I could do about it. There was no longer a power struggle because I had no power. I had rendered myself helpless, and I knew it. This shock of reality made me grow silent.

I hadn't realized it had all been a precious gift that should have been handled with more care, not something due me because I was "better" than everyone else. Now my beloved career was flying out of my hands like sand in the wind. Gone were those great times of hovering the aircraft or taking off with a formation, the camaraderie of being part of an elite group, or the joys of seeing a soldier do well. All that hope of a future military career and those plans of retiring as a colonel, or better, were gone. I had no one to blame but myself. When I left his office, all I could hear was the sound of my own military boots connecting to the tile, as if they were telling me with each step, "You are walking away from what could have been a really great career."

I was immediately moved over to the post headquarters to do some nonessential office job while waiting to be moved out of the military. Cruz was given the chance to go to Korea or get out. Because I was the higher ranked officer, I was held to a higher level of accountability and subsequent punishment. Just like I mentioned before, "From everyone to whom much has been given, much will be required; and from the one to whom much has been entrusted, even more will be demanded"

(Luke 12:48 NRSV), here was that higher level of expectation. Since the commander had given warnings to me personally, and not to Cruz, he held me responsible for not coming clean. Cruz had seventeen years in the military (twenty years qualified him to have one half of his final basic pay for life) (Office of the Secretary of Defense, Military Compensation, Active Duty Retirement System; http://militarypay. defense.gov/retirement/ad /index.html), but he decided to get out and hopefully fill the rest of the time with National Guard time or Reserves so we could be together.

Cruz was relieved to be out of his failing marriage and excited about a new start. He had gotten married at 18 when his wife was fifteen and pregnant. He felt he'd lost some of his youth by marrying her. He felt that he'd done the best he could but that it was time to go. Like me, I don't think he fully realized the changes our decisions would bring about. At first he didn't act ashamed or like this was a negative thing. I think he wanted to stand by his decisions as if they were honorable. He saw taking his responsibility for our baby as important, but somehow at the time he hadn't quite thought through leaving his other children. The fact that his ex-wife got involved with another man and thought she was pregnant before our divorce was final seemed to help his guilty conscience. Her boyfriend was not a healthy choice for his children, nor did she have the means to provide for them, so he decided that his children should move in with us. That way he wouldn't be abandoning any of them, just his ex-wife. Cruz's retirement plan was ok because the National Guard always needed maintenance pilots. In the beginning, we were like a team fighting "them," the army and our ex-spouses. The depth of changes to his life hit him slowly in the first year after his military career folded.

I remember meeting up with my OH58D lieutenant and platoon leader one day during the informal investigation. He was a really good man, pilot, and officer who was humble and respected. All of the 58D guys were humble men since they had to support the more prideful attack guys. I always respected that platoon. He asked me if it was true, but I couldn't tell him the truth face-to-face. I was too ashamed. Since we were drawing down the unit, I figured that he'd never know the truth if I denied it. I lacked the virtue of fortitude to speak in truth.

"Woe to those who hide deep from the LORD their counsel, whose deeds are in the dark, and who say, 'Who sees us? Who knows us?' You turn things upside down!" (Isaiah 29:15 RSVCE). Instead I denied it and told him that I was just going through marital trouble. Just like the brigade commander, I feel badly about leading him astray. God forgive me and bless him, as well. I was so far from the Lord, so far from Truth, that I hid it even from myself and those I respected.

The baby made us think about marriage. We thought it would have been a tragedy if it had all been just for fun and not for a real relationship. We both wanted it to be worth all that. After all, our officer evaluation reports had said we were shining examples of honor and integrity. Weren't we still?

Back then a divorce in that state only took three months. I remember meeting Jason at the courthouse in August. It was a reality check to see Jason in such an impersonal place with a judge between us. We met briefly in the parking lot after the divorce, talked with each other tearfully, and hugged one another. It was the last time I ever saw him. Even today my heart aches to speak of it.

I was asked to do one last job as a captain in the U.S. Army on the day I was processing to leave. I was in the office that processed soldiers coming in from other units to start their assignments at Ft. Hood. The noncommissioned officer who was handling my out-processing asked if I could help him. His own officer was out of the office, and he needed a captain to swear in the new young soldiers and pin on their rank. Some of them had their whole career ahead of them in the Active Duty. I remember looking intently at each one of them wondering what they would do, where they would go; wishing for them a full wonderful career. It nearly broke my heart. I loved the military, and I had put my all into my career. To leave it this way was heart-wrenching. I suppressed my tears at the time but let them flow as soon as I left the building.

We got married by a justice of the peace on September 17, 1995, when I was four months pregnant. She married couples in her home; an old, 70s style ranch that hadn't changed much in 20 years. Pregnant and now showing, I walked down her narrow hallway like it was an aisle and got married in her kitchen wearing a dress I had found at J. C. Penney's the day before. Our maid of honor and best man were a maintenance test pilot and his wife, friends of my new husband's. I didn't know either of them well. There was no music, no joy — it was horrible. Why would it have been anything else? We hadn't even asked God to come to the ceremony, nor would we have thought to do so.

CHAPTER 3

Hitting Bottom

*O*ut-processing and our next steps happened simultaneously. There was barely time to breathe. First, the military put us in contact with a seminar for job placement in the civilian world. So in August, before our final papers were even drafted for out-processing, we were driving up to Chicago to this seminar. There was no time to sit around the apartment enjoying quiet down time or even to get to know each other more in a home environment. We had little time to even reflect on what had just happened in our lives, as we were running from one thing into the next. It wasn't until we were settled that we had time for that. I didn't know it then, but a ticking time bomb was waiting for us in that future reflection.

In the little time that we had, barely a week, we were invited a few times to the homes of soldiers we knew. The first to invite us was a wonderful Samoan island man who was our First Sergeant (1SG). He had flower necklaces hanging from his van's rearview mirror and a beautiful, kind smile. He always made me feel as if he had inner peace and had just come off the beach. Somehow I knew it was because of his faith. He was like the father figure of our troop. From time to time, we went together; he, the first sergeant, and me, the commander, to talk with or get one of our soldiers out of jail. He always handled such situations with a loving yet stern hand. I felt as if it was our time for just that. He and his wife had us over to their home to listen and help in any way they could. And a few of the crew chiefs (enlisted maintenance soldiers) from our unit had us over one evening to just talk and also give us an open door. I was amazed at their kindness and genuine caring.

Oddly enough, though, I felt worse with the first sergeant and his wife than I did with the soldiers, even though they looked up to us and our rank. The soldiers were living together without being married and did not have the moral standards of the first sergeant. The soldiers accepted our affair as normal, and this almost appeased our guilt. I didn't want to let the first sergeant down. He had been my co-leader with these very soldiers, and now I felt as if I was the one he was visiting in jail. It was humbling to visit with him, even more so that he was kind, given our situation. We were completely honest with him, but more self-righteous with the soldiers.

The first sergeant and his wife asked us what our plans were. They wanted to know what would become of us. We told them about our upcoming interviews in Chicago that held great prospects. We were both naively hopeful, possibly because we had not known the insecurities that the civilian workforce had to face, having been protected from them by the military most of our adult lives. The reality of job finding was not really a concern for us, as if it was a sure thing. In many ways, those days flew by as if we were in a daydream, floating along like we were in a quasi-type of life.

The seminar we attended in Chicago was put on by a placement agency contracted by the military. They brought in prospective companies looking to hire former military leaders. Jealousy and frustration in the mirror of reality that started to be revealed erupted between us in the nights in the hotel as we prepared our interviews and resumes. A good number of companies wanted to interview me, but Cruz was not getting the same response. He became angry and wanted to leave. I knew that this might be our only avenue to bridge the gap to the civilian work force and didn't understand his anger. I understood his frustrations, though. He didn't have a full degree and was applying for maintenance management jobs. I, on the other hand, had management experience, a hard BS degree, and commissioned officer time. I also had the advantage of being a woman, thereby giving companies the opportunity to fulfill their discrimination requirements. I looked perfect to the hiring agents, but Cruz actually made me turn down some interviews. The people in charge were amazed, and so was I.

Again my feelings surfaced like back when I did the laundry for us the first time. My thoughts reeled. "He must just be frustrated from all that's happened. He just doesn't see the reality in front of us somehow." I hated how he let his feelings control the situation instead of considering what was best for us, like he was having a temper tantrum. He made me feel guilty for even wanting to interview and go back to the seminar. I began to doubt myself, asking if it was right for me to press forward for those interviews. It was a mind game that I did not want to play, and it made me angry and frustrated.

This experience was an opposite reflection of my past. I had often had opportunities like this knock on my door, but I'd never had someone trying to keep me from them for selfish reasons. In fact, most everyone had tried to help me and encourage me, even when it wasn't the best choice for me. This negative, controlling authority was foreign to me, especially in the face of positive decisions. I didn't like it, and it made me more and more uncomfortable with him. It was as if the pink sunglasses of immature, new love, or at least what I thought was real love, had been torn off, and now I was seeing a bit more clearly. I didn't like what I saw. It frightened me, and yet the possibility of getting off that train before it wrecked didn't cross my mind.

Loyalty and devotion was the only thing I could think of. Or perhaps it was pride. I did not want to admit I had made a wrong choice, and now it's ugly thread was weaving its way in the tapestry of my life. Just like when Jason and I walked away from the woman who was being hit by that man during our walk, I would pretend it wasn't real, wasn't a problem. It's interesting that what bothered me in Jason then, I was now doing to protect myself. My, how justification weaves its way into lies! Little did I know at that time that Cruz's behavior was only the tip of the iceberg. Nor did I know that the way he treated me would slowly whittle away at my resistance.

One day Cruz was so angry that he didn't even go to the seminar but stayed in the hotel all day until I returned. He really just wanted us to leave. But I went in anyway and spoke with the managers of the seminar and asked could they find a company that was looking for both production managers and maintenance. I told them a little about our situation, and they said they'd talk with some of the companies that were really interested in me. They came back excited that a supplier to the auto industry located in the northern Midwest wanted me very much, and, yes, they were actually thinking about filling a maintenance supervisor position, as well. They wanted to interview Cruz, too.

I was so excited. I went back to the hotel to coax Cruz to come back to the seminar for the interview. He finally agreed and did a great job. They said they'd pay for our move plus three months of our first rent to help us get us settled in. They even flew us up to look at the company.

Soon we were leaving the military and entering the automotive world, Cruz as a maintenance manager and me as a production manager. They hired me even though they knew I would be five months pregnant upon starting.

We returned to pack and tie up loose ends. We rented a U-Haul with a hitch for his Camaro. On the way down, Cruz drove the U-Haul and I drove my MX3 Mazda sports car with one of the kids. Cruz refused to share the route, wanting me to just follow where he led, but sometimes we got separated by other cars. The farther we got, the more frustrated I became at his not letting me see a map. It was crazy, and I let him know it when we finally stopped at a McDonalds. By then I was furious. We got into a big argument in the parking lot. I took my wedding ring off and flung it, telling him that's what I felt about his trying to control me. He ran and got it, tried to calm me down, and finally shared the route with me. We got back on the road and tried to forget the whole thing.

The dark cloud of authoritative control I had experienced in Chicago during the interviews and over the laundry incident was back. My harsh reactions and resistance to it was not keeping it away; in fact it seemed to be inviting more. Although I kept pushing it down, I felt the darkness settle in. Something even scarier was certainly coming.

Soon after we got settled in our new home and jobs, I had another big change in my life. I became a parent . . . but not to a newborn. Before their divorce was final, Cruz's ex-wife, Betty, got into an affair that was unhealthy for her and her children. Not that we were showing a healthy lifestyle either, but sadly we were the better choice at the time. The boyfriend carried a loaded gun and kept it around their apartment, drank a lot, and did drugs. Soon we heard that her new boyfriend was physically abusing Betty. Could it be that she was unconsciously repeating what she'd experienced for years with Cruz? No, I didn't even want to think that way. In all of her sorrow, jealousy, and anger, she'd reacted by finding someone who treated her even worse, who would lead to even more sorrow.

As far as I know, she had been faithful to Cruz throughout their marriage. Cruz even said she was a good mother but argued that her intense involvement with the children left him feeling outside much of the time. He was the one who had committed adultery against her just as I had done to Jason. The anger and hurt she felt about our affair, our sin, tempted her to sin, which caused more pain and trouble. "Whoever divorces his wife let him give her a certificate of divorce. But I say to you that anyone who divorces his wife, except on the grounds of unchasity, causes her to commit adultery; and whoever marries a divorced woman commits adultery" (Matthew 5:31-32 NRSV).

Now she was making unhealthy choices for herself and her children such as sleeping with a man before marriage in a drug and abuse filled environment. There is a reason why our Lord tells us it is not good for us to have sexual intimacy before marriage. It is a sin because it causes a loss of integrity, not only in the couple engaged in the act but within the individual. "The chaste person maintains the integrity of the powers of life and love placed in him. This integrity ensures the unity of the person; it is opposed to any behavior that would impair it. It tolerates neither a double life nor duplicity in speech." (CCC2338, sighting cf. Matthew 5:37) "Chastity includes an *apprenticeship in self-mastery*, which is training in human freedom. The alternative is clear: either man governs his passions and finds peace, or he lets himself be dominated by them and becomes unhappy." (CCC2339) *"Fornication* is carnal union between an unmarried man and an unmarried woman.

It is gravely contrary to the dignity of persons and of human sexuality, which is naturally ordered to the good of spouses and the generation and education of children. Moreover, it is a grave scandal when there is corruption of the young."(CCC2353) All of this was true of us. There was grave scandal and corruption of the young. We hurt others by our choices.

Betty was extremely angry with us and remained unforgiving and malicious throughout our whole marriage. Not that I blamed her, but hers was an unholy wrath that was damaging not only to herself but to everyone involved. In her affair with this man, she was partly trying to make Cruz jealous. She dressed provocatively when they made a switch with the children before we left and told him she thought she was pregnant and needed his help. He even took her to the hospital one night out of guilt. We went as far as paying her full child support for all three children while the kids lived with us so that we could help her get on her feet.

She tried every angle to frustrate our marriage. She plotted to turn the kids against us, sent locks of her hair in perfumed envelopes to Cruz trying to make it look as if he was still in love with her, and many other things. "He who commits adultery has no sense; he who does it destroys himself. Wounds and dishonor will he get, and his disgrace will not be wiped away. For jealousy makes a man furious, and he will not spare when he takes revenge. He will accept no compensation, nor be appeased though you multiply gifts" (Proverbs 6:32-35 RSVCE). This was exactly true of our situation; we were destroying ourselves, jealousy and doubt were aroused, Betty became a thorn in our side and nothing we did abated her anger.

At first, I didn't feel guilty about their divorce because their marriage was in trouble before I came along, but I did feel guilty about her state in life after Cruz and I were married. At the time, I didn't relate to stay-at-home moms never having had to work. I almost wrongly felt as if she had been taking advantage of the situation. So in my mind, I somehow erased my guilt, but I did feel bad about her being separated from her children.

Cruz said she had secretly wanted to get pregnant with their last son, now four, because Cruz had told her that he might leave her. She didn't want to go to work or know what she would do if she had to. Somehow Cruz's justification for why he was controlled into staying in his marriage longer because he helped get his wife pregnant made sense back then to a self-centered mind such as my own. After all, didn't he join in on making that child? Hadn't he been open to loving her during that act and to the life that could possibly come from it before doing so? Or was he merely doing it for self-gratification and pleasure?

What kind of justification can you bring to not wanting the fruit of life and the commitment to it before intimate sexual union in a marriage if it's merely only selfish desire? Doesn't marriage say that you want to give yourself completely to another, that you have decided these things and are open to them so that the union between you is clear? If it means these things, having a child to control one's spouse would never come into the picture as a possibility. What did sex mean to Cruz when he made that comment about marriage and Betty? What had it meant to me then, and what does it mean now? This was the duplicity in Cruz's speech referred to in the CCC, but I didn't know it then. Did it mean that he also felt controlled by our baby growing inside me? Was the sex only for the moment and not making a statement about unity? All of this came crashing in on me.

I had never used sex to control him even if it was before marriage, but neither had I thought out the fact that I was making a physical promise of unity forever to this man by doing so. I, too, was using duplicity in speech in this way, not being "the chaste person that maintains the integrity of the powers of life and love placed in me that ensures the unity of my person."(pag73) I was also in the moment of the pleasure without seeing the future promise I was making with my body, saying one thing with my body but not actually meaning it or even thinking it through with my mind, heart or soul. How could I point a finger at Betty when I was not holy in my own actions?

Because Betty had been only seventeen when they got married, she had never worked. But now that she only had child support to maintain the lifestyle they were accustomed to living prior to the divorce, she needed to get a job to supplement that lifestyle. Jason went back to school, got his teaching degree, and started a career teaching history along with his coaching, but Cruz's ex-wife found herself at a loss. So because of all this, and the problems with her new boyfriend, Cruz decided his children would live with us until his ex-wife could get on her feet, and she agreed.

As you can imagine, the kids seemed to almost hate me. They were twelve, ten, and four, and I had the most trouble with the oldest girl, Beth, at first. Her mother would call, and the kids would take the phone into their rooms and close the door so they could talk. One time I found my earrings in the toilet, and another time I found my military memorabilia strewn around the basement with some of it missing or broken. We later learned that this was silent, hidden anger prompted by their mother. Years later Beth told me that they all had a play in this mischief, but I never felt I could blame them for it. I knew where the source of the anger and hurt was coming from.

But because Beth was also a good soul, and I really tried with her, she slowly started to soften. She never tried to run away, or speak disrespectfully to me, but at times she had a sullen look, one that said she was just getting through it. She got involved with school, had good friends, and good grades. As time went on, she was a very good girl. She just needed time to heal, forgive, and sort it all out for herself. Once in genuine tears I talked with her in the kitchen about how badly I felt about the separation I caused between her parents. It helped us to bridge the gap. I didn't know anything about things a teenage girl needed, and she was probably too embarrassed to ask me, so we never really went shopping or did girl things together. I just didn't have a clue. Now I feel badly about not helping her more in that area.

The second oldest had a hard time, too, a boy who was also named Cruz, but he internalized most of it, which seemed more dangerous. We tried to get him involved with baseball teams and playing in the orchestra, but his grades slipped badly. He was mostly quiet, whereas at least Beth would talk. He was hard to reach. It was very hard on him. The youngest was the easiest, a happy little guy who we called Buddy, and yet he really missed his mom, too.

They were lost children. I understood their pain to some extent, but I could not put all the pieces back together for them. Their mother's sorrow and jealousy caused more trouble with us because in her anger and hurt she would call and stir up the kids on purpose. The stress in our new family was so thick you could cut it with a knife.

I felt badly about how I had misled the colonel and the lieutenant, but I felt serious remorse toward these children in spite of and maybe to some degree because of their hatred toward me. Gone were the carefree flying missions. I knew nothing about raising children, and Cruz had left most of it to his wife. Not only that, but I was pregnant with all that entails: nausea, fatigue, bloating, emotions, and swelling, all coupled with starting a new job.

Soon Cruz started competing with me at work. He had been assigned to the night shift while I was allowed to stay on day shift. While on the night shift, a lazy, gossipy old manager who had been moved to nights because of problems he had started on days put the notion into Cruz's head that I was not a good manager. He didn't even know me, but Cruz's jealousy over me being left on the day shift, and the memory of how we got the job in the first place, made him vulnerable to this man's gossip.

When Cruz finally got back on days, I would find him hiding behind pillars in my department, watching to see if I was talking to any of the men under me. I believe the whole thing had left him feeling insecure as the man of the family and provider, feeling he'd lost some status or respect. Maybe it was even partly as if he was again in the situation of me being a higher rank, just like in the military. But I wasn't outside of myself enough to even think of these things so that I could talk with him about it. I just felt attacked and unsure as to why it was happening. He would come into my office wanting to check the personal files I kept on my employees. Naturally, I refused to show them to him. We had silent anger toward each other over such things, not being able to put them into words.

Soon after his office hired summer college help who all happened to be beautiful, young girls. If I walked by his office or went into his office to talk, one of these girls was invariably sitting on his desk, swinging her legs, laughing and talking with him. I felt jealous, too, especially me big and round with pregnancy while these girls were so thin and young. When I talked with him about it, this only created more tension in our relationship. Our trust of each other was about zero because of our record with our own spouses.

Soon the day came for our son Billy to be born. He was a beautiful, ten-pound boy with long lashes. We called him Billy after General Billy Mitchell of WWI. Known as the father of the air force, he was a pilot and commander in the army. Billy's middle name was Dean after Cruz's grandmother, and my own great grandmother. Billy was a light shining in the darkness. He was a happy baby, always cheerful and playful. He was full of an innocence that was lacking in our lives.

Going back to what I knew from my past, I wanted to get him baptized, but Cruz was an agnostic. On his mother's side, his Catholic grandfather had repressed his Jewish grandmother's religion during WWII. Also his parents who had been Catholic had their own problems with the authority of the church over contraception and left the church all together when Cruz was small. From this, he had drawn his own conclusions about the Catholic faith. He wanted his child to make his own decision about what faith to be baptized into when he came of age. I kept trying to get him to agree with me though I wasn't sure what baptism really meant or why infant baptism was important to me. I just knew it was something important to the Catholic faith.

I have since learned that "Following St Paul, the Church has always taught that the overwhelming misery which oppresses men and their inclination toward evil and death cannot be understood apart from their connection with Adam's sin and the fact that he has transmitted to us a sin with which we are all born afflicted, a sin which is the 'death of a soul.'(CF. Council of Trent: DS1512) Because of this certainty of faith, the Church baptizes for the remission of sins even tiny infants who have not committed personal sin. (CF. Council of Trent: DS1514)" (CCC 403) Baptism is the start of our Christian initiation because it is recognition of Christ's grace made available to us from his passion and resurrection made possible through the Sacrament of Baptism, which washes that original sin away and starts us on our journey. That's why baptized infants require faith-filled parents to nurture this gift of grace as they grow. We need Christ at our start so that His Holy Spirit can be deposited to give us a chance to be cleansed and to belong to Christ and His body from the beginning. As my life shows, life is hard enough, even with the Holy Spirit. We should give our children all the chances for His grace God has given us through the sacraments. Even with my own uncertainty, I battled over this with Cruz for two more years, largely because of our own faithless lifestyles.

After Billy was born, we started attending the Catholic mass from time to time with all four children. It still amazes me that Cruz came to those masses for me. I think that he, too, was searching for peace and thought possibly he might find it there somehow. We were looking for peace to find us like some fairy dust that just happened to be sprinkled on us. Jesus was waiting for us to come to Him with contrite, repentant hearts, but still we did not surrender. Things had to get steadily worse before we saw our need to do this.

Cruz was able to get back into the National Guard about this time. This offered a small ray of hope for him. He could be back by the aircraft he so loved. It meant that he wasn't going to lose the lifetime retirement benefits that would come with all his years of service. But even that would soon be taken from him.

After Billy was born, I lost all of the weight right away and had curves for the first time in my life. This didn't even really occur to me, because I spent all my time with my new child, and soon I was back to work. But Cruz became more and more jealous and started to drink hard liquor heavily.

His drinking was kind of undercover. He'd have the hard liquor on top of the fridge. When I noticed he was starting to drink more, I started to privately mark where the alcohol was the day before so I'd know just how much he'd drunk, and I'd be prepared for the worst. Sometimes if it was near the bottom, I'd even pour some out, so he wouldn't drink as much. We just didn't talk about it at all. But when he drank, his personality would change to despondent yet angry at the same time. He would get drunk at home and become physically abusive toward me. The kids were never touched, thank God.

Jealousy I believe many times is acted out by accusing others of the temptations one has and or is acting on. I believe his jealousy was like this, a way of acting out his own feelings. He felt he'd made a mistake, was ok with his divorce with his first wife, but wasn't at peace now and didn't even have his beloved army career to hide in. He didn't like working in automotive. He found it to be mundane and not exciting as flying the Apache and being on the move all the time. Life was closing in on him. He had to blame someone because when he looked at his own fault in it all, he started to feel insecure. Some of the insecurity likely came from his own childhood, as well, with his own father being gone much of the time on active duty.

Jealousy is driven from insecurity and a lack of knowing one is loved. Even without the liquor, Cruz was controlling because of ungodly jealousy. He accused me of trying to look good for men at work while he was putting on skin makeup and spraying his hair with hairspray so he could look good for the girls or for anyone really, to show he was more than what he felt inside. It became so bad that he would not allow me to have friends or even speak with the neighbors. Even my family was a source of contention. One time when my brother and his wife came to visit, we argued about his not wanting them there. Cruz went to a hotel, not wanting to be part of my family in any way. He did not want me to have any outside connections or support.

Our schedule was hectic. We got up around 5:30 am, and I ironed his shirt for work while he showered. Then I got the two youngest kids up for daycare and dressed them. Then I got ready and took the kids to daycare while Cruz drove directly to work. I started to feel as if I was doing everything by myself. Cruz hadn't shared in childrearing with his first wife because she was a stay home mom, but I was working, and it wasn't the same. Even though this was all new to me, my mothering instinct had kicked in, and I wanted to ensure that the kids were comfortable and loved. But I was wearing myself out, especially right after having had Billy and going back to work so soon.

The littlest things made Cruz angry like if he thought I'd been gone too long at the grocery store, if I asked for his help with house chores, or if I was busy at work and asked him to pick up the kids. He was drinking hard liquor more and more. I could tell when he was drinking because he would usually listen to really loud hard rock music in the living room and be in a foul mood. "It is not for kings to drink wine, or for rulers to desire strong drink, lest they drink and forget what has been decreed, and pervert the rights of all the afflicted" (Proverbs 31:4-5 RSVCE).

He started demanding I bring him a glass of water or a drink and rub his feet while he lay on the couch. Once I challenged him about him expecting me to wait on him, and it erupted into an argument. He pinned me down, strangling me, and then forced me to sit on the floor with my back to the wall, waiting until I was ordered to get him something. When he demanded a drink, I got up and got him a glass of water. I remembered watching the TV series about slavery called *Roots*. One time, one of the slave women who was at a well had to do the same thing, and she spit in the water. Out of anger, I did the same, and served it to him while I took my place back at the wall on the floor.

There were many other times like these, very physical. He dragged me up the stairs once by my hair, played Russian roulette with a bullet in the pistol, making me sit in the shower with him. He closed all the blinds and pulled the phones out of the wall so that I could not call for help. It was mostly when his kids were gone, and Billy was sleeping. One time we were in the car together, a Suburban. We'd had an argument that morning that was still smoldering. After dropping Billy off at daycare, the other kids were at their mom's at the time for a visit, he was driving really fast on the ramp to the highway, swerving so that the car started to tip, saying he was going to kill us both. He wanted me to stop him, almost as if he was showing me what would happen if I argued back on any issue like I had that morning.

Another time when his kids were there, they heard us arguing in the bedroom. They also heard loud bumping sounds as Cruz threw me to the ground, and I tried to defend myself. They questioned their dad, and as always after an altercation when the kids were there, he had a group meeting to alleviate his guilt. He sat us all down in the living room so he could explain away *our* actions, as he put it. He did not address the physical abuse but denied it, explaining that adults had arguments sometimes and that was healthy. Beth, the oldest, came right out and said she remembered once when he had been abusive to her mom in the car, pushing her face back and forth across the dashboard. She knew what was really happening. But, embarrassed, he denied that incident strongly saying it never happened, just like he did with us. He never apologized to me, not once, until years later.

The power struggles of the long ago laundry incident, the interview in Chicago, and the argument over the map on our road trip were nothing in the face of what was erupting now. The warnings God tried to show me about the unhealthy controlling authority of the warlords back in Somalia had fully erupted in my own life and marriage. I hadn't heeded His warning signs along the way; His gentle pressures during the dance.

Now my life was like a slow death. I was no longer fighting for power or status. I was in survival mode, both mentally and physically. I could no longer deny the reality. It was right in front of me, as real as it gets, but now there were differences. I had a child from this union, and I had experienced his children's pain from our actions. To turn away from it all meant more defeat and loss of meaning for all our actions. Pride kept me from realizing just how weak I was and in need of God's healthy secure authority. Some of us have to hit bottom before we are ready to surrender to His way, so He can build us up into what we are meant to be. I silently swallowed the grief and pain of our horrible marriage, trying somehow to find some kind of normalcy in it all.

Not long after the family meeting after the abuse, the kids all left for a time. Beth went to his parents, and her brothers went back to their mother's. That left no one to explain his behavior to and a worse situation for me, but I was grateful that his children were out of our environment.

At times when the abuse was bad, or he'd been drinking, and I was afraid, I'd call my mom. She was a refuge for me, a thread of safety even if it was only on the phone. But I didn't call her all the time because I knew I'd just go back and try to make it work, and when it would happen again, I would be embarrassed to call her again.

I felt as if this whole thing was payback for my affair and lying about it to the army. Why would I ever deserve more? It was like the old saying, "You made your bed. Now you have to lie in it." I hadn't understood that God was loving, wanting me to stop hurting myself, wanting me to come into His shelter of warmth and security by surrendering in free will to His will. I still thought I loved Cruz, knowing the fun we'd had. The whole thing was such a shame. I felt that if I left him, the whole thing would be for nothing. Failing my marriage after having to leave my beloved army career was just too much for me to accept. I knew the transition from the military was probably harder on him than me since he had been in for seventeen years and I'd only been in for seven. All of this made me feel that I deserved whatever tough times we were having. Having the baby changed my thinking about divorce. I wanted us to make it work, to be a real family.

It may be hard for some, even for myself, to understand the extreme poles of power I have experienced. I went from being a commander in the attack Army Calvary to being an abused working mother. After much thought, I believe I ended up on both ends of the spectrum because of my deep-rooted sense of needing to be self-reliant in all things. *I* had to fix my problems and make them work, no one else. I was so driven by this that I thought somehow I could keep it all together, even in an abusive situation. Self-reliance had had its talons in me from back in college when I had a hectic schedule to the work I did in the military, making my husband Jason follow me, and especially when I was in the role of attack commander. Self-reliance was proving itself to be an unsafe authority and a poor guide.

I thought problems were meant to be overcome and that those who failed were weak. I didn't want to accept weakness or need, only strength. Not that God wanted me to go through the horror of abuse, but God wanted me to see my need for Him. He would use what the devil meant for bad for my good. "But He said to me, "My grace is sufficient for you for My power is made perfect in weakness" (2 Corinthians 12:9 RSVCE). With problems like I was going through, God was asking me to identify His role in my life. "And He said to them, 'But who do you say that I am?' And Peter answered, 'The Christ of God'" (Luke 9:20 RSVCE). But my answer did come out like Peter's. I didn't really know God as Christ, my refuge and strength, a forgiving, loving God. I thought I had to be my own strength, as if God was far from helping someone like me who hadn't really loved Him all that much. I did realize fully that He came for the lost, but I didn't accept that I was lost because that would mean that I was not in control of saving myself. I think that's why counseling scared me so much and turned me off when Jason asked me to go.

But the abuse got so horrible at times that I would run with Billy, barely escaping in the car. One time when my parents came to visit, my mother went upstairs with me and handed me a small piece of paper with a phone number and a name on it. It was a safe house to run to if I needed it. She told me to put it in the back pocket of a pair of pants on the top of my shelf, someplace where he wouldn't suspect it. She knew I could not have private things in that house and knew she couldn't make me leave the situation until I decided to. I hid it like she told me.

About a month later, I had to use that number and moved out to the safe house with Billy who was only four months old. Cruz had gotten abusive again horribly, and I knew from the reminders from my mother's visit that I needed help, that it was ok to call out for help. How different I was now from the long ago self sufficient soldier in Somalia smirking at others in their weakness. In the one chance I had when he was out, I got Billy, a few clothes, bottles, and necessities into the car and left.

The safe house was under cover so that abusive men could not find their victims. Cruz had taken my wallet, my identity cards, and all the credit cards, anything I could use for independence, everything of liquid value available to me, even the bankcards, leaving me with nothing. His determination to leave me helpless was without bounds. He monitored me every second, leaving me no time to sell anything for cash or to divert my direct deposit so as not to go into our joint account. But eventually he had to leave to get food, and when he did, I left with no ID or means to access money, just the gas left in the tank.

In the safe house, I had one room with a twin bed and a crib for Billy. Other than that, the room was bare, but it didn't matter. I didn't have anything, anyway. The first night was cold in that big, old house with its many rooms and people I didn't know. I was quickly put to work cleaning the bathrooms for my stay. I remember feeling embarrassed to ask if I could have a few diapers just until my next check came. Because I'd taken the Suburban, they thought it looked as if I was rich and told me it was only for those people who didn't have the means. In my frustration, I cried out to the woman who worked there, saying, "I can't get to any money. My husband's taken my ability to access any existing bank accounts, but I have changed the account for my next paycheck, and I'll be able to pay you back when I get it. Please, I am not trying to take advantage of you." It was all so humiliating to me.

Her eyes softened. She opened the door to the storeroom full of baby supplies and said, "Sorry, but judging from your vehicle it looked like you were better off than the rest. You can have whatever you need." I wanted to crawl into a hole somewhere and disappear. Was this really me, the Calvary attack commander with a degree in mathematics and good job? How did I end up here with these other women? I didn't want to be connected to them, but I was. It was so surreal.

This was part of hitting bottom. I needed to feel the bump of absolute helplessness, even though this was still not a big enough bump. Even writing this, it amazes me just how much I fought to stay in self-reliance! How much it takes some of us to see clearly. How much we struggle in sordid surroundings though we are princesses of a King meant for so much more! O, God, forgive us our trespasses against Your gentle knocking, calling in love and guidance to safe provisions.

At that time, our company was moving from one side of town to the other, so Cruz and I were working in different plants. This allowed me to work safely without his constant presence. But he could come and go in the plants as he liked, so this arrangement was tricky to maintain. I had to leave work to get Billy when I was fairly sure he'd still be at the other plant, drive out of my way to make sure he didn't see us, without using too much gas, and then get back to the safe house. By the grace of God Cruz was so busy at the maintenance management job during moving that he had no spare time to come looking for me all the way across town. It was ok for the time being, but not for long, just until I got the next paycheck deposited in my own name. Then I would have to look for somewhere to live. Eventually, time and space seemed to make his abuse less real, and I started to fall back into those old feelings of trying to make it work again.

While I was at the safe house, I saw just how bad some situations get. One woman's husband tried to burn her alive, and she had the scars to prove it. We'd sit around after our meals and talk. It was like group therapy, though the things they shared were hard to hear. But even these stories didn't scare me out of my self-reliance. I wasn't at the safe house long because I couldn't get past the feeling that I wasn't like these other women. I was educated, had a job, and still believed that I could fix things, so I called him from a secure line after a few days. "Where are you?" he asked. "Can I see you? We can work this out. I love you. I want us to work." He was nice, convincing, and almost apologetic in his own way. Within a week, I had moved back home.

The abuse stopped for a little while, but soon it was back in full force. Once when it got bad, I put Billy in his baby seat and drove to the Catholic Church down the road from our house because I knew I'd find sanctuary there. I went in the dark church, lit a candle, and knelt down to pray. I was sobbing, and by grace Billy had fallen asleep. I didn't know what to do or where to go, and I felt terribly alone. I needed answers. The janitor, an older, gentle man with white hair, came in and saw my distress. He was so kind and with a sincere look on his face he asked, "Can I be of help to you in any way at all?"

"Oh, I'm sorry, sir, I am so lost. I'm with an abusive husband, and I've just run out the door for safety," I replied. "I really don't know what to do, so I came here, I think for answers and to pray somehow."

"Why would you want to stay in that environment?" he asked. I told him that I didn't really want to leave him, but that I didn't know what to do or what was right.

"I don't think God would want me to run from my problems and break up this family with a separation and divorce. I have messed up so much already. I think I should try to work it all out, don't you?" I asked.

"I'm not sure," he answered, "but I can see what you're saying." He offered me a place to stay for the night with him and his wife. I told him that I had to face the problem, that I didn't want to run away from it. He was not pushy but gentle like our Lord and extended an invitation to me to call him any time I needed to. God sent me an angel that day as love reached out to me in my time of need, like God calling me to His peace, only I wasn't ready to accept it just yet.

Instead, I went back time and time again, feeling that I had made this decision and that I could fix it, or maybe even that I deserved it because of the affair. I have often felt that his abuse and drinking was his own guilt coming through. Possibly in a strange way by punishing me he could somehow get rid of the horror of all we had done. The abuse continued to grow worse along with the control. Several times he tried to strangle me, leaving bruises on my neck as I struggled to get him off. I often started to faint before he'd pull away. He'd just say, "Why don't you put some makeup on that?" as I was getting ready for work the next morning. Another time he was running after me upstairs. I had Billy in my arms, so I ran into the bathroom because it had a lock on the door. I pulled the drawer out by the door to block it so he couldn't open it even if he did unlock it somehow, which he did. I put Billy in the tub and found a few things for him to play with while I waited it out. He was yelling threats through the door, laughing at my attempts to keep him out, saying he could break the door down if he really wanted to. But he didn't. I looked at the window. We were on the second floor, too high to escape. I could yell if I needed to but that would be involving someone else, and then I wouldn't be able to stop the train of events that would follow. I decided to stay in the bathroom for a few hours, waiting for silence, waiting for the car to start up, waiting for his anger to abate. Eventually, he calmed down, went somewhere, and we came out. Reuniting was always awkward. We acted as if nothing had happened, silent, just being in the house together until eventually things evolved into a more normal setting.

I could barely breathe in that home. I'd come downstairs at night when the house was quiet and sit alone at the kitchen table just for some peace. Otherwise, I was never relaxed or at peace except when I took care of Billy when Cruz was out of the house. In between the times when there wasn't abuse and things were better, we were still sexually intimate with each other. It seemed to be an attempt to repair things or apologize to me for the abuse. I felt even more alone after these times, knowing it wasn't going to last and that it was not a reflection of reality. It was another mind game twisted with softness. This marriage was a far cry from what God intended a healthy growing nurturing union to be. Neither one of us felt it.

God does not want us to punish ourselves for past sins. He came so that we would have life and life to the fullest. If we believe in His saving power of the cross through our desire to be forgiven, we can be set free of our past mistakes and sins. He is even able to redeem the effects of our sins on others we have hurt through healing and time. But we need to trust that He is the good shepherd leading His lost sheep back to the fold.

The devil wants us to think that there is no hope after taking the apple and living in the consequences of that sin. But Jesus came so that we may have hope for tomorrow. "I am the door; if any one enters by Me, he will be saved, and will go in and out and find pasture. The thief comes only to steal and kill and destroy; I came that they may have life, and have it abundantly. I am the good shepherd. The good shepherd lays down his life for the sheep. He who is a hireling and not a shepherd, whose own the sheep are not, sees the wolf coming and leaves the sheep and flees; and the wolf snatches them and scatters them. He flees because he is a hireling and cares nothing for the sheep. I am the good shepherd" (John 10:9-14 RSVCE).

Constantly punishing myself for my past sin was not and is not God's plan for us, but neither is divorce an easy escape. He wants us to come to Him for forgiveness, to repent of old ways, and, yes, do what we can to make our sin right with those we have hurt, but He does not want us to continue in physically hurtful situations caused by sinful choices. It is like a drug addict going back for another hit, thinking he is never able to rise above his first choice of sin. It is a wrong thought process. God hates divorce; the answer wasn't divorce but surrender to God. "They said, 'Moses allowed a man to write a certificate of dismissal and divorce her.' But Jesus said to them, 'For your hardness of heart he wrote this commandment for you. Therefore what God has joined together, let no one separate.'" (Mark, 10:4-5,9 NRSV). He did not bless this abuse, nor was it a healthy union in the first place.

The Church is actually quite clear about this. The Code of Canon Law in No. 1153 §1 states: "A spouse who occasions grave danger of soul or body to the other or to the children, or otherwise makes the common life unduly difficult, provides the other spouse with a reason to leave, either by a decree of the local Ordinary or, if there is danger in delay, even on his or her own authority. Regular mistreatment is a violation of justice and charity; it is a wrong that should be resisted and, with the help of God's grace, righted." Two wrongs, my decisions and this abuse, didn't make a right. Although God doesn't like divorce, He doesn't want His children abused either. It was man who forced the union, not God, but God was the only one with answers. He was calling me to surrender to His way of healing and peaceful pastures.

During this time, Cruz' sister Jamie and her two young girls moved out from the west coast for a job. I liked her. She was humble, having gone through her own hard times, and at the time was down-to-earth and loving. I never shared with her what her brother was like, but I had the sense that she probably would have believed me if I had. She was the only family either one of us had within 500 miles. She was allowed to come over freely, so it was a release to have another soul to befriend.

Our family and my sister-in-law's family had all planned to go on a picnic together on a Saturday afternoon. Cruz wanted to make potato salad for the event himself; it was not normal for him to be in the kitchen at all, so he wanted me to peel the potatoes, boil them, and have all the ingredients out for him to mix up. When he finished, he left everything out and laid down on his spot on the couch without a word, expecting me to clean up the mess and put the salad into a bowl for the picnic. Something in me that day had just had enough. I hadn't gotten a lot of sleep the night before, it had been a stressful morning, and my patience was running low. As I started to clean up the kitchen and put the potato salad in a bowl, I decided to make an audible, sarcastic complaint about feeling disrespected. "I guess I'll just clean up in here, too, while you lay down on the couch."

I think he was ready for that comment. He exploded with anger, saying I never appreciate anything and started to run after me. Billy was in the living room on a blanket. He couldn't walk yet but could kind of roll around. I tried to grab Billy to protect him, but Cruz grabbed Billy out of my arms and ran and picked up a hammer. Then he put Billy back in the living room on the floor, separating him from me. I didn't run then because I was worried what he was going to do with Billy. He forced me into the front room and started to physically strangle and push me down on the floor, yelling at me the whole time. He said he was going to kill Billy because I must love Billy more than him and that he would kill me, too. While hurting me with the hammer on my lower body he inadvertently hit my nose in the process as I struggled to get free, which I think helped me because seeing the blood caused him to stop. It was bleeding all over the place. I tried to push him off of me, but it only made him more furious. When he ran into the living room to get Billy, I escaped out the front door and went to the neighbor's, screaming for him to call the police.

Our area was a new neighborhood, so the neighbor's house was about a block down the road. It was cold with sleet and ice on the ground. I'd run out there in my stocking feet not even thinking about how I looked with the blood all over me. The first neighbor was in his garage with the door open and just turned around and went inside his house trying not to be involved, so I ran to the next home. I knocked on the door frantically asking for help. The man who came to the door looked at me like it was a dream but called the police.

Worried about Billy, I immediately ran back to the house, and as I was doing this, the police got there. The police station was only 1.2 miles away, really close to our house, and thankfully they must have been in their car close by. I was screaming to the police as I ran into the house, "My baby, my baby, he has my baby, and he might kill him!" When we ran into the house, I saw Billy creeping around on the living room floor, looking for his momma. I ran to him and hugged him, kissing his whole face, telling him how much I loved him. Cruz had taken his old '76 Chevy Camaro SS and driven off.

The police asked me some questions, got my story, and checked to see if anything was broken or if I needed emergency care. I told them I thought I was ok for the moment. They asked if there was anywhere I thought he might go, and I told them probably his sister's place. They asked me to get into their car and guide them over to her place. We drove quickly and found Cruz leaning into the trunk of his car. He had just changed into the military fatigues that he'd had in his trunk for his next weekend drill. He probably changed because he figured that the police would be looking for a guy with blood on his clothes fitting the description of what he'd been wearing before he changed. The police handcuffed him and took him to jail. He didn't fight them, just stayed in his position leaning over as they pulled his arms back and put the cuffs on.

The police officer told me that I should go to the emergency room and get checked out so that there was an official report of my condition.

The hospital felt cold, and the nurse was rough and mean, as if I was making the whole thing up, but the doctor was nice. They made a report.

I went to a hotel that night. I could not yet go back into that nightmare of a house so soon. I called my mom and let her know what had happened. I also called Cruz' sister and told her that her brother had been arrested for physical abuse but not much else.

We ended up having to go to court. The investigating officer said he had never, ever come across a man so controlling and manipulative as Cruz had been with his responses and comments while being questioned. Cruz was an intelligent man who knew how to use emotion and personal comments to manipulate a situation, leaving the other person reeling with confusion. At first, he came across to others as honest, fun, and genuine. You just wanted to believe him. He'd explain things in such a way that it made you think he might be right even though you knew the thing was wrong. Like the time during our interviews when he tried to convince me that the people at the job seminar were being discriminating toward him and that we should just both leave. I knew they weren't and that we needed the jobs.

My mom and my sister Mae came to support me during the trial. My father was sick of the whole mess, and I think he wasn't sure what he thought, so he stayed to take care of the farm and go to work. The trial was hard for all of us. The judge told me he would grant anything I wanted. I told him I didn't want to keep Billy from his father altogether but that I didn't think it was safe to leave him alone with him for now. I requested that he have chaperoned visitations at the minimum. Other than that I just wanted to have the assurance that Cruz would not come near us without consent. This he immediately allowed.

Cruz was put in jail for a short time and then on probation for a year after that. We received a Personal Protection Order (PPO) that prohibited Cruz from having any contact with us at all. As he was leaving the courtroom, he tried to give me a stuffed animal he had brought for Billy, but my mother intervened. I was so lost and sorrowful, and yet a part of me felt safer than I had for over a year. We moved Billy's crib, a mattress, some pots and pans, a few dishes, and the table and chairs into an apartment. I only wanted the necessities from that place, nothing more. And so Billy and I started to heal and get back on our feet.

Our general manager at work called me into his office asked if the allegations were true. The police had sent the report of the situation. He told me he had had a similar situation in his extended family and wanted me to know he supported me. He had fired Cruz because having the two of us working together just wouldn't be healthy for us or for the company. He asked me to let him know if there was anything he could do.

But the feeling of not being able to fix this situation haunted me. I couldn't shake the belief that this failure was weakness on my part. Cruz was my last connection to my old life, to the military, and even that was going away. I wasn't ready to surrender it altogether. Having Billy also changed how I saw the whole thing. Though I couldn't let it go, I had not yet thought about asking God to help and guide me for the long run. I still hadn't learned that God is strong in us in our weakness when we surrender to His care.

All of these troubles with Cruz made me reflect on Jason and my first marriage, what I'd left behind. I hadn't taken that marriage seriously. In fact, I took it for granted. The line from the Joni Mitchell song "Big Yellow Taxi" is true. "You don't know what you've got til' it's gone." It was easy with him compared to how hard it was with Cruz. At times it made me long for Jason's easy going friendship, but that was long gone, something I'd thrown away like some old worn out shoe. But this marriage was still hanging on, within my reach. There was a big difference in the passion these two men had toward me. Cruz's passion was the opposite of Jason's indifference. I wanted passion mixed with compassion and easy going friendship.

In time, I called Cruz's sister to ask how he was doing, and she said he was out of jail and wanted to see me. I shouldn't have done it, but I agreed to talk to him, and soon we had a meeting. Cruz told me he'd been to church, had been praying, and had changed. He wanted a second chance and swore that it would be different. This was the first time I ever felt that he saw what he was doing and that it was wrong. Cruz's softening and his seeming regret over his actions were a thread of hope, and I wanted to believe. I wanted it to be true. He was my husband. So I allowed him to come over, and soon he was sleeping overnight and staying with us.

After he got out of jail, he had gotten another job as a maintenance manager at a little automotive supplier shop for awhile until he could find something better. But, this was with a break in his pay and the addition of the new apartment rent, we were hurting financially. So we moved back into the house and made another try. Even his boys moved back in with us because their mother was having serious troubles with the man she was living with. It was hard to believe and very sad that we were the better choice for them.

We were barely making it before he lost his job, but now it was even worse. Cruz had a lot of credit card and department store credit debt when we got married. Along with the house payment, the car payment, and his child support, we had over $5,000 in payments per month. We paid child support to the kids' mother even though the kids were living with us, partially because we still felt guilty. This added an additional burden of jealousy and loss of income. We barely made our payments. In fact, we were falling behind, leaving little left to live on. I was still renting out the house Jason and I had built, but the rent didn't quite cover the mortgage, leaving us with about $50 left to pay per month. Cruz hated that I still had that house from my past and wanted to get rid of it. In addition, I had brought about $5,000 worth of my own debt to the marriage. We were drowning in credit debt and expenses. "A man who builds his house with other people's money is like one who gathers stones for his burial mound" (Sirach/Ecclesiticus, 21:8 RSVCE).

On top of all this, Cruz wanted me to quit my job because it made him feel badly that they knew our story. I didn't want to quit. I loved my job and was comfortable there where it wasn't stressful. But I really wanted to make this work and make a new start, so that's exactly what I did. The time loss from my changing jobs and having a pay cut at first further drained our finances. Our debt was around $60,000 without the mortgage or cars included. It was largely credit card debt. We were only able to pay off the interest with a bit of principle if we were lucky. With the added $860 child support check we sent out monthly, this put our monthly outgoing money at around $5,100 in bills alone, not to mention we still had to heat the house and eat. Our take home at its best was about $6,000 a month, leaving us with only $900 for food, utilities, gas and whatever else we needed. With the kids, I spent about $800 in groceries alone so we were really falling behind just paying off interest on the cards. Each month we had to decide which credit card we would pay off and which one we were just going to pay interest on. It left me feeling sick to my stomach every time I sat down to juggle the bills. With all the debt, we decided to file bankruptcy on February 10, 1997. I was horrified. I had come from a farming family that was wise with money and spent only what they had. Our financial state furthered the stress and anxiety we had in our home. On the outside everything looked great. We had a nice home, nice cars, and cute kids, but on the inside, it was slow self-destruction.

One weekend to get out of our rut, we all went to a nearby air show. We walked around looking at the aircraft and enjoying what we used to know. Cruz went over to the hangers, but it was a far walk, so I stayed back with the kids. While he was there, he met up with a soldier from our old Calvary unit. It was the very same soldier I'd counseled for having an affair with another soldier's wife; there he was still secure in his career. They talked a long time about our whole situation. The soldier asked him why I was such a hypocrite to counsel him and yet do the same thing and lose my career. There wasn't anything to say other than that he was right. Cruz came back and told me how hard it was to speak to him. It seemed to make all we'd lost come back in our faces, and for what? Stress and misery. We were trying to work at it all but not making very good progress.

Cruz had kept going to his once a month weekend drills in the National Guard, but because now that he had a felony on his record, he wasn't legally allowed to hold arms or handle weapons. Since he had been an attack helicopter pilot in the military, and all soldiers need to bear arms anyway, this meant he could not meet the responsibilities required for his role. He was told he no longer could fulfill his time because of his record and was out processed. This really hurt him because he had only two and a half years to go to get retirement for the rest of his life. This furthered his stress after our financial struggles. Right around then, Cruz got a new job with better pay at a bigger company, we were only too happy to have him be accepted even with a felony on his record. Happy for the moment that is, because this company with its connections would have a final permanent negative effect on our marriage.

Then I became pregnant right away with our second son, Raphael. Our intimacy was so infrequent that we didn't have contraception on our minds. We hadn't even thought it would be necessary, as if Billy had come as a one in a million chance. We named him Raphael John; it was my wish for a name after Raphael the Archangel, one of the defenders in battle from evil, and John after his father's middle name. Raphael came as a surprise and an uplifting distraction to me from all the negatives in our lives. I was happy that Billy would have a brother to grow up with, happy about another new beginning. I knew this baby would bring more of the only joy I had known in our home that which I'd experienced with Billy. I welcomed this new child with open arms. I knew it would mean more financial burden, but to me the joy of new life far outweighed any financial difficulty he would bring.

Cruz was not so happy. Though he loved his children and welcomed this new son fully, he again felt trapped, weighed down even heavier than before. Cruz said he didn't want any more children and wanted me to get my tubes tied as soon as I had the baby. Because our marriage had been so stressful, I decided he was probably right, though I really loved having children, and it went against my grain. I hadn't questioned why he didn't getting a vasectomy instead because our doctor said that the procedure could easily be taken care of at the hospital right after the birth and would be covered under insurance. Our insurance covered tubal ligation, but I did not know then that it would not cover the roughly $20K required to reverse the surgery if I ever desired it. Nor did I know that even if I had that reversal it didn't fully return me to how I was before. At the time, I didn't plan on being with anyone else in the future. I hadn't stopped to think of the moral implications or statements I was making with this decision. I merely wanted peace between Cruz and me in the present. I didn't even really fully realize that this decision was a permanent one that would affect me for the rest of my life.

I didn't tell my parents about it, which shows that I had some lingering doubts that I chose not to investigate because I thought they would only cause me more frustration. Right after having Raphael, they wheeled me into another room for surgery, and my tubes were tied. It was such an unemotional process for such an important event. I was wheeled in, received anesthesia, fell asleep and then woke up to have the gift of life blocked inside me for the rest of my life. I can't even say I felt remorse at that point, just a kind of emptiness that stayed with me. I stuffed it deep inside not wanting to know that it bothered me. But it would and did bother me like a smoldering fire that would build over time in my inner being.

The two boys are twenty-three months apart, Billy being about nine months old when Cruz was picked up to go to jail. I worked for one year at a die shop, scheduling their production while I was pregnant. It was the only company that would hire me while I was pregnant. There was a manager down on the production floor I had to get information from that was a Christian. He was a tough man, hard worker, but fair and good. He wasn't embarrassed to talk about his faith. He talked with me from time to time about God's love. It was as if God was reaching out to me, telling me He was near.

Things with Cruz were stressful again. It was no longer physically abusive but mentally controlling. The physical abuse dropped off because he knew if he did it again that the prison sentence would be much, much longer. But the mental part was fair game, something no one could see or prove. Slowly the dialogue between us became nonexistent, as if I had done something wrong and was being given the silent treatment.

One day I was in a car accident coming home from the die shop on a Saturday. I had brought Billy with me because I only had to pick something up and then come home, and Cruz didn't want to watch him. I was about seven months pregnant with Raphael at the time. We hit a car that stopped suddenly in front of us, and it jarred us, me in the belly and Billy bit his lip. The car was totaled. I called Cruz at home to ask if he could come get us. I was shaking and really upset. He just responded that he wasn't feeling so well and that we would have to take a taxi or something. That's just what we did. He didn't even care if we were hurt or ask about the car. It was my problem. Cruz was distancing himself from all of us now, not just physically, but emotionally and mentally.

Again I felt like a prisoner in my own home. It was emotionally draining. There was no laughter between us except for the children, no fun. I think losing his retirement, the added stress of another baby, the financial burdens piling up with the pending bankruptcy, the other kids living with grandparents and their mother, which made him feel guilty, all started to cave in on him. Partly he blamed me. Partly I blamed him. Counselors say that any one of those things causes stress in a marriage, but we had them all.

In spite of this, we drove out to the farm to be with my parents for my birthday on December 13, 1997, a month before Raphael was born. It was the first time we had been to my family's home since we'd left the military. The time there went well, but on the way back and when we got home, the old stress flooded in.

It was like he was trying to show everyone he was good to alleviate his guilt over the past. If he treated me nicely in front of my parents, or anyone else, possibly they would think he hadn't really abused me and that I'd made it up, that he wasn't really as bad as the sentence had said he was. Looking back, it was almost as if these family visits that he allowed "all of a sudden" were to put us on display to erase doubt in anyone's mind that he was a good husband. Maybe on his part, it was even an attempt to start over. I think it was a false statement to family of his innocence, even if it was subconscious, because the stress in our home when everyone else was gone became even worse.

To this point, we even went out to his parents on the west coast for Christmas only a few weeks later. While we were there, a cousin of his who was the same age came over. He sat with her the whole night out on the deck talking about how bad I was and how much he wanted out. They came back in both looking at me like I was some kind of outsider and monster. The whole time we were there, everyone treated me like a second-class citizen, prompted by him. He was their son. I began to take on the guilt in their eyes of our past and his felony. Again the truth was being twisted. Here was that old duplicity, loss of integrity and loss of unity from CCC mentioned previously and all stemming from the father of lies. Marriages should be bonding and supportive, but we were separate and against each other.

After Raphael was born on January 14, 1998, I left the die company and returned to management in a wonderful automotive plastics company led by a good Christian man; it was God again showing me I had not been forgotten. This company was like a breath of fresh air, so supportive and a new start, but Cruz couldn't let that be good for me. I started on a job that had twelve-hour rotation shifts, so I worked three 12-hour shifts one week and had four days off, and then worked four twelve-hour shifts the next week and had three days off. This meant that sometimes I worked weekends and that sometimes I was off during the week when my husband was not at home. It seemed like a good solution to me.

Once Raphael was born, I went back to my old weight, and he soon became jealous again of the other men who worked with me since he didn't know them. He wanted me to quit or transfer within the company to somewhere else so that I was not on the twelve-hour shift. I hated to leave that job because I really loved it, and the people seemed to love me, too. But to keep the peace, I put in for a transfer.

Soon after the transfer, things at home started to get really bad. I was home more, which is what I thought he wanted, but it also the very thing that caused more stress. Now I was there to feel the control, to feel the guilt he piled onto me. We had many long debates from work over the phone, by email, and especially at home about my hours, who I was working with, taking care of the children, picking them up if I had to stay late at work, how this was not good for our family, and on and on. He couldn't control me when I was at work, and it didn't sit well with him. When we worked at the same company, our schedules were fairly similar and he was in the know about my whole life. But now he had to trust that what I said was real . . ., but he didn't. I never thought about his work or the people he was with. It didn't occur to me to worry about it. Maybe he focused his jealousy on my work because eventually at his own there was a person there who changed our situation drastically.

Typically, he would come home and then go down and work out on the exercise equipment with the music on. So when Raphael was sleeping, I'd go down with Billy and put him in his play car to push himself around and try to work out with Cruz so we'd be together. He'd ignore me, not a word, not a look, even if I'd tried to talk directly to him.

Most of the time he wouldn't even eat with us. He was disconnecting, but making sure I was the one to handle the house, the chores, and the kids. Other than working out, the only other thing he did was to sit in that same couch and watch TV or listen to his old 70s hard rock. It was a little like I did with Jason. But unlike me, he still had passion about what I did, which I found strange. He still didn't want me to have any outside connections, even with my family, though he could do all this. I really never knew where I belonged with him in this time. We had some fair days, but mostly bad ones.

At this time, Cruz was still in touch with a man he had worked with at his old company just after he got out of jail. I think Cruz connected with this man because he was separated and living in the basement while his wife and kids were living upstairs. He had a problem with control issues, as well. He was a short, stout man with a sharp nose, an unkempt look, and mean eyes. I didn't like him the first time I met him. Once Cruz invited this man over to our home, but just before he came, we got into an argument. Cruz wanted me to be submissive and to come down and serve them and act like everything was ok, but I just couldn't do it. The two of them talked about me as if this man were coaching him in how to tame the shrew. It infuriated me. Also this guy had brought over a baby blanket for Raphael as a baby gift. Cruz told me that I was being rude to our guest, but I was not sure how to act given the situation. I sat upstairs and tried to pray, asking what to do.

At that time, I still didn't recognize prayer as a lifeline. I thought of it more as something you cried out for in the moment, not something that could change a whole life situation. These prayers were my first baby steps toward realizing that my self-reliance was not working. I sat upstairs trying to decide what was right, not just for me, but for everyone. In the end, I decided to go down and apologize for not being more hospitable. They both sat there smugly like they'd taught me a lesson, saying that I did the right thing. I kept it inside, quietly hating every smile, every moment of hospitality until he left. Of course, nothing was mentioned after he was gone, as if it never happened. It seemed like there was always a mind game afoot from Cruz, some type of "lesson" he was teaching me, trying to show how control was his husbandly right and duty. He wanted a dictatorship not a team. He was still drinking, but seemed to control it better, as if he knew it was a powder keg that would explode. The whole thing was like a teetering car hanging over a cliff, just waiting for a slight wind to push it over.

What had I gotten myself into? During the hardest times, I would call the Catholic Church I had been to earlier just to talk to someone. My baptized soul knew somewhere deep inside that the church was a refuge, but I didn't fully realize that meant that Christ was my refuge. Christ cannot be separated from the church, or the church from Christ; they are of one body with Christ as the head. "Christ is the head of the church, his body, and is himself its Savior" (Ephesians 5:23 RSVCE). But at the time, all I knew was that it was a safe place to run to. I didn't want to bother my mother. After what I had put them through, I felt too ashamed to let my parents know that things were not better or to tell them what was really going on.

Years later I received a vision in church and a dream about Jacob's ladder from Exodus 28:12 that went together and explained my actions and His calling me through His church. The vision came as I was deep in prayer during the consecration of the mass. Jesus was bound to a pillar right in front of me, right there in my pew. His back was to me and I could see His wounds just being whipped. They were white, and the blood hadn't flowed in them yet. He looked at me silently, His eyes full of sorrow and pain, and yet with so much love for me. I will never forget the feeling of His eyes piercing my soul that day. I wept uncontrollably in church. This vision told me He had died for me and that He loved me, but that I had to allow His redemption and His blood to flow into my wounds to knit back together all the injuries my decisions had caused. I had to learn how to trust in Him and His ways. His forgiveness was waiting for me, but I had to receive it. I needed to turn the knob on my side of the door and fling it open as an answer to His calling.

My dream about Jacob's ladder is recorded in one sentence that helped me with this vision to see how to receive His love and forgiveness. "And he dreamed that there was a ladder set up on the earth, and the top of it reached to heaven; and behold, the angels of God were ascending and descending on it!" (Genesis 28:12 RSVCE) The angels in my dream were singing beautiful music. In my dream I seemed to be somewhere on earth at the bottom of the ladder. The melody was strangely familiar, but to my frustrations, I didn't know the words, so I couldn't join in. Over time I started to learn them, as they came to me, I am filled with immense joy to be part of the praise toward heaven. Recently I came across this verse in Revelations 14:3 (RSVCE): "And they sing a new song before the throne and before the four living creatures and before the elders. No one could learn that song except the hundred and forty-four thousand who had been redeemed from the earth." These words, "no one could *learn* that song except the redeemed" jumped out at me. Though I had been redeemed, there was much I still needed to learn to sing the song of the redeemed and those angels on Jacob's ladder. I had to learn to work with the cardinal and theological virtues of prudence, justice, temperance, fortitude, faith, hope and love so that I could learn the song of joy. The best place for me to learn this song was His church where I would find guidance in how to live the virtues.

In her book, "The Mystical City of God," Sister Mary Agreda tells of a vision she received from the Holy Virgin Mary that the rungs of Jacob's ladder were the cardinal and theological virtues and that the ladder itself is Mary and the holy church she represents. The theological virtues of faith, hope and love are given as grace, but they have to be responded to or they will be lost. The cardinal virtues are gained through habit by repetition. God was showing me that I had to be in His Way, through His church with His Mother and His saints to learn how to do this. At times learning the virtues is like a death; almost like suffering because the old self fights not wanting to surrender its old ways. The more we die to self the more we open ourselves to God, His peace and His holiness. "And though the Lord give you the bread of adversity and the water of affliction, yet your Teacher will not hide himself any more, but your eyes shall see your Teacher. And your ears shall hear a word behind you, saying, "This is the way, walk in it," when you turn to the right or when you turn to the left" (Isaiah 30:20-21 RSVCE). I was just realizing how much I needed something other than myself, that I needed a soft, caring, loving, gentle Savior. The melody of heaven and His voice were whispering to me, but for a while, I would continue to drown it out with the struggle of self-reliance and kept closing the door to His calling.

About this time Cruz's boys had moved back in with us temporarily. One day we were all together shopping at a department store for Christmas gifts. Cruz's oldest son, Cruz(named after his father), who was about thirteen years old then, was picked up for shoplifting. We heard a call over the intercom for Cruz to come and get him in their office. They told Cruz that he'd smuggled a scope for a BB gun out to our car in his pants. They had it on tape. They didn't press charges but just talked with him before we took him home. Talking it over with his dad, I thought there should be grounding or some type of punishment for his actions, but Cruz didn't want to do any of this. He said that just talking with him was enough. But after talking it through with me, he also decided that a few chores around the house wouldn't be bad to show him we thought it was serious.

Cruz let the kids stay up as late as they wanted to if they didn't have to go to school the next day. The next night, his son Cruz and his little brother, Buddy, stayed up late and left the downstairs a mess with dirty dishes, food, clothes, and pillows lying around. So we left them a note to clean up. Normally, I would come home from work at lunch to fix them something or take them out to eat if they were home from school like this on Christmas break or during the summer. That day I came home to the same mess from the night before. After the seriousness of his stealing, I thought he would take it more seriously. I told him he'd have to clean it all up before we could go out to eat. I thought this was reasonable. The boy got angry with me, called a friend, and started telling him how stupid I was, using vulgar language to explain me to his friend. I wrestled the phone out of his hand, told his friend he'd call him back later, and told him to clean up right then. He started to yell, saying that I hurt him when I took the phone from his hands and that I was abusing him. He locked himself in his room and wouldn't come out, so I called his dad.

Cruz said he was busy at work and couldn't come home though I told him it was serious and he should come home right away. He came home, went into the bedroom, and got his son's side of the story, never asking me for mine. He came out believing I had hurt his son. As I tried to explain what really happened, his son yelled at me saying, "She's lying. Just look at her face." I was incredulous at the whole thing.

Later when Cruz and I were alone, he said he didn't think it was going to work out between us, that the kids were tearing us up, trying to put a wedge between us. I didn't think it was the kids at all but our trust in each other that was lacking. The whole thing with his son still hurts my soul to this day. I loved his son enough to try and teach him that stealing wasn't ok and that cleaning up after himself was his responsibility. I wanted him to know that he was worth showing that to.

Later his son Cruz did the same thing to his father when they were alone camping, yelling that he'd abused him. Cruz was incredulous and told me about it, apologizing for not supporting me more about this incident. He wanted to share my innocence in how his son reacted, wanted others to see he hadn't hurt his son. But how could we expect any less from children who had been in such confused homes full of abuse between the parents?

Soon after this, my husband started behaving strangely. He started to work out more, focusing a lot of attention on what he looked like. He went to rock concerts and did not return home until late. And he continued to be very distant with me, like I didn't exist. I started to suspect that he was seeing another woman. One day, I found a piece of paper with a phone number and a woman's name on it and called it. It was a home phone number. She answered with, "Hello," but afraid and not wanting to really talk, I hung up. It made me even more convinced.

At this point he was a maintenance manager again, working for a new, larger company. Then he told me that he had to go on a business trip to Las Vegas and needed to go shopping for clothes. I supposed it was possible that he had to go down to the proving grounds near Las Vegas for a maintenance meeting, but I questioned it because he'd never gone before. Since he was fairly still new there, it seemed like it was all right. We really didn't have the money to be sending him on a trip to Vegas. He'd have to pay for the trip up front and be reimbursed, but he said he had to go.

Just before he left for Vegas, he told me that he wanted a divorce. He wanted me out of the house by the time he got back. I was devastated because I knew this wasn't something I could fix again. He said that with all of the past stress and the thing with Cruz, his son, that it was all too much.

I remember sitting in my car in the parking lot of a department store with the Bible in my hands before going home from work. I had grabbed it knowing it was holy and full of God's answers, but I was not sure how to get them from it. I asked God if He thought divorce was an answer for me in spite of what I had done. I told him I realized now that divorce was wrong, but asked if it was ok for me to go along with this divorce. I finally wanted His advice instead of charging forward in my own messy way. Without knowing scripture well at all, I opened the Bible randomly and it opened to these verses. "If any woman has a husband who is an unbeliever, and he consents to live with her, she should not divorce him. For the unbelieving husband is consecrated through his wife, and the unbelieving wife is consecrated through her husband. Otherwise, your children would be unclean, but as it is they are holy. But if the unbelieving partner desires to separate, let it be so; in such a case the brother or sister is not bound. For God has called us to peace. Wife, how do you know whether you will save your husband?" (1 Corinthians 7:13-16 RSVCE). The answer from the Lord was clear. I was not free to divorce unless he left. But he *was* leaving me. In fact, he said that he wanted me out without discussion before he got back. I asked him what about his own children, he told me to take them with me until he returned. I believed that he had already left me for another woman. I decided not to fight the divorce request, though it hurt me to my core for yet another failure.

His two boys were still living with us and somehow the oldest sensed things were about to change again for all of us. He started to be gentler, nicer, and softer with me, wanting more time, asking if he could help out. This was the same boy who'd accused me of hurting him. My mother always told me that truth would come out and that in the end kids know who really loved them and cared for them no matter what they'd done. While Cruz was still in Vegas, I decided to spend the few days I had left making it fun for the boys. I knew the chances were high that neither their brothers nor I would ever see Cruz's kids again. It was a bitter time of forced smiles and fun through sorrow. I had done most of the caretaking of these boys for the last three years and loved them as my own. I felt horrible about how their lives had been affected by our poor decisions. They were like the lost boys from the movie *Hook*.

I took them sledding, then out to eat where there was a play place, and later we watched movies. The last night came before we were to move out and their dad to come home. The oldest who I had had troubles with just a few weeks before for stealing asked me if we could all climb in bed with me for the night. I could see how uneasy and insecure he felt about what was happening. He just wanted to feel safe, loved, and secure. He knew I loved him, and in spite of my part in the affair that ultimately caused his parent's divorce, amazingly, he loved me, too. Oh, how easily children love, how harshly we hurt them in divorce, and yet how quick they are to forgive. Oh, how I wish even now that I could change time and the decisions of mine that affected them. The last I heard the oldest boy is now married with kids of his own, and the youngest is having a rough time though he has finally graduated from high school at nineteen years old. The girl who lived with her grandparents is also married with two children and has told me she and her husband are back in the Catholic Church regularly. Lord, please bless these adult children and their families.

By the time Cruz got back from Vegas, I had moved into the new apartment with my boys. His older boys and Beth stayed with him at first and then after a short while left again to live with their mother and grandparents. Billy was about one year and three-quarters and Raphael had just turned a year old that week. I know Cruz wanted to keep and take care of his older boys, but as soon as I moved out, his girlfriend Terrie moved in, causing a bit of upheaval and change. Beth had mentioned to me one day that they'd been together. I thought it was possible, so it didn't shock me. Cruz eventually told me she'd moved in, so I knew that it was just a matter of time before I'd be facing this woman when I took my boys home to visit their dad. I later found out that the woman I'd called that day was a buyer for his new company. With all of their phone conversations at work, Cruz had started to like her, and the next thing I knew, she was moving into my old house.

Here I was moving into an apartment again at 33, with only a car, which would soon be gone because of the bankruptcy, and no furniture, except the kitchen table, the hutch, a mattress set on the floor for me, and the boys' beds. I had no respect, no family, no credit, and no joy — definitely no joy. By the grace of God, I did, however, still have a job at that great automotive plastics company owned by that good Christian man.

CHAPTER 4

Building up from the Ashes

*T*imes were tough for us there at first. Since I had to be at work at 5:40 am, I had to have the kids dressed and at daycare beforehand so I could get there in time. Backward planning meant that I had to be up by 3:30 am at least. Those were long days. Managers were expected to be at their jobs not for a mere eight hours, but until the job seemed managed, which usually meant ten hours or more. I normally left work around 5:00 pm. It was a long time for the kids to be at daycare, and it was hard on me, too.

One morning at 4:30 am after my shower and changing, shortly after moving in, and before I was able to find an affordable car to replace the Suburban, I was just plain exhausted and tired of my life and what I had made of it. Gone was my great flying career. I had a horrible track record — two failed marriages and ruined finances, not to mention the loss of respect from my family, especially with my father. Feeling empty and defeated, I thought about the whole mess as I sat at the kitchen table with a small light on, not wanting to disturb the boys in their warm beds. I reached out for the big, white family Catholic bible my parents gave me when I first got married after college. I had kept it all those years, knowing it was the Word of God and knowing I should respect it. I hugged it close, knowing He had heard me before when I turned to Him for answers. I hoped that if I just held it close that maybe God would hear me again, maybe He would see fit to give me some morsel of His mercy and a listening ear, though I knew I didn't deserve it.

Through the sorrow and exhaustion, I called out to God. "Please show me where there is joy in my journey. If it weren't for the boys . . ., I just . . ., I would just want to die." And I broke down really for the first time since the first divorce and wept for all that I had done, for my sin and all that it had cost everyone and for where it had left me. I was so tired of wrong choices. The burdens were too heavy. I was reaching out for Jesus to yoke Himself with me.

What I had not realized up to that point was that I hadn't really considered the journey along the way. I had such tunnel vision. It's like driving to get somewhere on vacation without stopping to rest or eat and then arriving all stressed out. God wants us to consider the journey along the way, for it is in the journey that we learn how to love Him more and to truly be in His family. One of our retreats at church refers to the journey as the dash between the date of birth and the date of death on a tombstone. What we do within the dash really matters! We can apply this to the big picture and all of our daily tasks and missions.

After I prayed about my journey, I got ready for work and went about my day. That afternoon I stopped at our local grocery store before picking up the kids. There were only about three people in the store at the time, which seemed odd. One of the three people was an elderly woman. I met up with her at the meat section, and she said something I found strange. "It has been one year since my husband passed away. We were married for many years. Today is our anniversary, and he always gave me a yellow rose on this day. I was praying that perhaps I would receive one today, and a man in the store just came up to me and gave me a single yellow rose. What do you make of that?" I didn't know what to tell her. We parted and the whole thing just stayed with me.

I had taken my diaper bag in because I was using it as a purse. The diaper bag was sitting open on the child seat part of the cart in front of me. After leaving the elderly woman holding her yellow rose, I wheeled down the canned vegetable aisle. There was no one around me the whole time I was in the store except the woman. I bent down to get a can, and when I stood up, I saw a green pamphlet that hadn't been there before on top of the bag. The pamphlet read, "Joy in the Journey . . . Maranatha!" I didn't know it at the time, but Maranatha means, "Come, Lord Jesus, come into my life." I left the cart and ran around the grocery store looking to find who had left it, but found no one. I knew it was God answering my prayer from 4:30 am that morning, maybe delivered by an angel. Who uses the words, "Joy in the journey" in normal conversation, anyway? I didn't usually.

The pamphlet was about a Christian women's retreat on the shores of Lake Michigan near Muskegon. It also happened to be one of the first weekends the boys legally had to go to their dad's after the divorce, which gave me an open weekend.

The divorce awarded me full physical custody with reasonable visitation, which meant that I had the kids all the time. We agreed that the boys would come to visit him on every other weekend. The divorce decree stated I should receive $916 dollars a month for the boys, but I knew Cruz wouldn't be able to pay that with his other child support and his life expenses. He talked with me about it asking me to lower the amount, so I decided to sit down with all their expenses as they were at the time and divide them in half. I didn't put in rent or utilities — maybe I should have. After looking at the expenses, I came up with $545 a month, which was what I figured would be his half of what I thought I needed to pay child daycare, diapers and food, the minimum. I wrote up a change to the temporary divorce decree pending and made an appointment with the court to ask them to lower it so that I was being honest and fair to his situation. They were stunned. They'd never had any woman lower the amount. Cruz said he'd raise it when he could and when the other children graduated, although this never happened. So now the divorce was legal.

We had decided that visitations every other weekend would be fair for him to start with. The first weekend they went to their dad's it was really hard to let them go. After dropping them off, I came home and sat in their room, hugging their stuffed animals, crying that they were not with me, that I didn't know this woman who would be changing their diapers, feeding them, and being their parent for two days. It is probably what Cruz's exwife; Betty, felt when I was her children's mother. It all came crashing in.

The boys were returning to the same house I had left, only now he was living there with his girlfriend. We never talked about his involvement with her before we were divorced, except once years later when he denied it. Somehow it didn't really matter to me. My real concern was that she would be good to the boys. Cruz assured me she would, but there was nothing I could do about it one way or the other. It was the law.

I knew when Cruz had the kids for the weekend that he loved his kids and would watch over them but I had no idea what their environment would be like. I remember going to pick up the boys after the retreat. Terrie answered the door with a kind hello and said she'd go get the boys and be right back. She then shut the door, leaving me standing on my old front steps. It felt strange as if I should run in and see what was going on, to see if Cruz was even there, but I stood waiting. I didn't want to even touch the handle on that old door. All I wanted was to get my kids out of there and be away from old memories.

Even in my immature faith, I knew that God had set me up that weekend to go to the Joy in the Journey retreat. I also knew if God had done this that somehow he would make it ok for the boys, too. In retrospect, I can see God was helping me get through this hard time. What a loving patient forgiving God we serve!

So I called to reserve a space for the retreat though it was quite close to the start date. When I called, the woman told me she didn't think there were any openings, but that she would check. When she came back on the line, she was amazed to report that there was just one spot left. It was like God had held it open to welcome back His lost lamb!

I was learning how to surrender to God's ways. A few years ago I went to a day retreat and learned that surrendering to God's authority is not like succumbing to a commanding leader. It is more about choosing to follow Him because it is healthy for you. This reminds me of what Jesus said to Paul when he was charging off to Damascus to kill the rotten Christians because he thought they were defiling the truth about God. "Saul, Saul why do you persecute Me? It hurts you when you kick against the goads." (Acts 26:14 RSVCE). Goads are prods used on animals that have a hurtful point on them. The animal's master does not touch the animal with the goad; rather the animal bumps up against the point when it rebels against the master's guidance. The goad produces a quick, sharp pain and can even pierce through the flesh if the animal isn't careful. Jesus was trying to tell me as clearly as He was telling Saul that I would just hurt myself if I kept going against His guidance. I had kicked against the goads so often and was in so much pain that I didn't want to fight any longer. I was beginning to see that His is the Way, the Truth, and the Life and that anything else would hurt me. God wanted me to be at peace because He loves me. "The Lord is my shepherd, I shall not want; He makes me lie down in green pastures. He leads me beside still waters; He restores my soul. He leads me in paths of righteousness for His name's sake" (Psalms 23: 1-3 RSVCE).

At the retreat, there was a speaker who had been divorced twice and then married a good Christian man. She talked about how God loved and pursued her through all her wanderings in her own desert. I began to see that God was pursuing me, too. I could scarcely believe that He still loved me, forgave me and was even pursuing me with real love even though I had behaved like the woman at the well. In spite of her sin, she became one of Jesus' first missionaries because she realized her need for Him and His forgiveness. "My denunciations were for the self-satisfied. For the sinner, who felt his failure and weakness, I had the tenderest pity. 'Go, and sin no more,' was My Word to the woman taken in adultery. But what a Word of hope that was, revealing as it did the assurance that I trusted her not to fall into sin again. That I deemed her capable of a new life. The Samaritan woman at Sychar's well I trusted with a secret that even My disciples had not shared fully with Me. She was one of My first missionaries. I recognize, too, the wealth of love in the offering of the woman who was a sinner. There was no public denunciation of her sin, no repulse of her love" (*God Calling II*, April 30th, edited by AJ Russell). This woman at the well was me. I had been publically denounced in my self-satisfaction in the military, but here now in my need, failure, and weakness at this retreat, Jesus was giving me that hope and trust so I would somehow learn the song of the redeemed, learn how to love, trust, and hope in Him in return.

On the break, a woman sitting next to me told me how God had showed her that He could be her spouse after the death of her husband. At first that didn't sit right with me, but as I thought of His innocent, selfless love, I started to understand what she meant. I had been the spiritual prostitute, leaving Him again and again for other things. He wanted me back, which was so unbelievable! I had never experienced that kind of love and mercy. Through His Son, God and the Holy Spirit were preparing me to walk that aisle to the heavenly gate, dressed in a beautiful robe of white, like at a marriage feast, so that I could be one with our Lord forever. His spouse is the church, the body of Christ, with Jesus as its head. He pursues us back to the wedding feast of the Lamb! "'I looked, and behold, a great multitude which no man could number, from every nation, from all tribes and peoples and tongues, standing before the throne and before the Lamb, clothed in white robes, with palm branches in their hands. Then one of the elders addressed me saying, 'Who are these, clothed in white robes, and whence have they come?' I said to him, 'Sir, you know.' And he said to me, 'These are they who have come out of the great tribulation; they have washed their robes and made them white in the blood of the Lamb. Therefore, are they before the throne of God, and serve him day and night within His temple; and He who sits upon the throne will shelter them with His presence. They shall hunger no more, neither thirst anymore; the sun shall not strike them, nor any scorching heat. For the Lamb in the midst of the throne will be their shepherd, and He will guide them to springs of living water; and God will wipe away every tear from their eyes'" (Revelations 7: 9,13,14 RSVCE). I was the prodigal son coming home to throw away the old rags I was wearing and put on the new robe and the ring on my finger. I was on the journey home. Joy in the journey!

I was so thirsty for everything about Jesus and His Way that I could scarcely be normal. I joined everything I could. A big non-denominational church only 45 minutes from our home and only 15 minutes from my work had sponsored the retreat. I signed up for a bible study right away. They also had a program my kids could be in while I was at the study, so we started to go every Wednesday night, and nothing but nothing took its place. I grew quickly as I learned His word. My poor study guides, I really put them through the wringer. I didn't let any "Why?" go by. I constantly asked questions. I was so on fire for all I could grasp and learn of this God whom I had known about for years but never experienced as a living God who was active in my life.

The veil from my blind eyes was starting to be peeled away. God wasn't concerned that I wasn't in the fullness of the Catholic Church yet. He is patient. He allowed me to be on fire in that place for a time, for a reason. "For everything there is a season, and a time for every matter under heaven" (Ecclesiastes 3:1 RSVCE).

The Holy Spirit was prompting me to forgive deeply in my soul. I didn't want to hold on to old feelings any longer anyway. I wanted the past to be healed; gone. I had to let His blood flow in to let the wound knit back together and make a new me. I started to pray for God to help me forgive and heal, as well as my ex-husband. "Therefore, I tell you, whatever you ask for in prayer, believe that you have received it, and it will be yours. And whenever you stand praying, forgive, if you have anything against any one; so that your Father also who is in heaven may forgive you your trespasses" (Mark 11:24-25 RSVCE).

One day I felt a stirring to bake banana bread in the scriptures I had read that morning. My ex-husband and his kids loved my banana bread. I decided to send the bread along when the boys had to go to their dad's as an offering of forgiveness and peace between us. I wanted him to know I was letting it all go, that I wouldn't be festering malice or hatred and that I wanted their environment, especially when the boys were there, to be one of love. "If your enemy is hungry, give him bread to eat; and if he is thirsty, give him water to drink; for you will heap coals of fire on his head, and the Lord will reward you" (Proverbs 25:21 RSVCE). So I listened to God prompting and sent the bread, which not only sent a message of love, but signaled my surrender and trust to God's provision as it went through that door with my boys.

Not long after that my ex-husband came to pick up the boys at my apartment. I invited him in to sit down while I was getting things ready, but he declined. We made small talk for a bit, and then there was a silence. Then he quietly said, "No woman should have had to go through what I put you through." I looked up at him, and he had tears in his eyes. It was so touching to me that the past hurt and abuse all melted away in that moment. I think he felt it, too.

I was so shocked at his unexpected kindness that I just remained silent at first, soaking in what I had just heard. Then I slowly raised my head as he was talking to give him comfort and to give me time to hear his words, looking across the room, I gave a small smile and said quietly, "Thank you. I'm sorry for my part in it all, too."

There were no feelings of wanting our marriage back, but God's Spirit was at work healing our wounds. He never again mentioned that day, nor did I. He never said he was sorry or ever acknowledged the abuse. But it was all I needed. God knew that, and I hope it helped heal him, too.

I continued to grow and love God more and more during this crucial time, the honeymoon of my faith. In many ways, it was a time of receiving, like a baby drawing milk from its mother. "For though by this time you ought to be teachers, you need someone to teach you again the first principles of God's word. You need milk, not solid food; for every one who lives on milk is unskilled in the word of righteousness, for he is a child. But solid food is for the mature, for those who have their faculties trained by practice to distinguish good from evil" (Hebrews, 5:12-14 RSVCE). I was too young spiritually to work on virtues of giving. During this time He was teaching me how much I was loved, forgiven, and called to His refuge.

God rained down blessings and gifts at this time, showering me with His love. I started to pray, not for others, but for things I needed and wanted. If I had been older spiritually, I might not have received these things like I did back then, so quickly, in such abundance. I didn't just get what I needed but what I wanted, "milk not solid food." God doesn't change, but we grow and change in what we ask for, receive, and give back, in how we perceive Him, His love, and provisions. The things I asked for back then, such as a flowered vanilla-colored couch, for example, would not be important to me today. Then I needed the basics, the milk. By the way, I still have that flowered white couch right next to me in my office as I am writing. It is an enduring reminder to me of those days. Since then I have come to know that He is with me always and that He is my provider come what may. I no longer see this just in material provisions. Now I ask Him to help me glorify Him in my need as long as He may want to allow it but that He please not give me more than what His grace will provide for. Now I see that "His way for me is not just a path of general righteousness and obedience, but the actual road mapped out for me, in which I can best help His needy world" (*God Calling II*, September 28th, edited by AJ Russell).

Having no car and no credit to buy a new one, I prayed for a car. I went shopping at used car lots with $1,500 to my name. Usually people need to be shrewd at such places because these dealers have a reputation for dishonesty. "The master commended the dishonest steward for his shrewdness; for the sons of this world are more shrewd in dealing with their own generation than the sons of light" (Luke, 16:8, RSVCE). So I decided to be strong. Finally, at one used car dealership called; Shortie's Used Cars, I found the car I felt God was pointing out to me. It was a white, 1987, two-door Volkswagen Fox with a sunroof and cloth seats. The sticker price on the car said $3,000. I knew it was the car I was supposed to have, but the problem was the cost and my credit. But I had such a strong confidence that this was the car God intended me to have that I was not worried in the least about how to come up with the rest of the money.

The son of the owner, a tall man (which was funny because of their name), in his late thirties to early forties, started to talk to me. I told him this was the car I wanted and that I had prayed about it. I explained to him that I was going through a divorce, I was a single mom and that we had filed bankruptcy and it had finalized only about five months before. I told him right away that I didn't have the money to pay the asking price nor the credit to cover the difference, but that I knew he would sell me the car anyway because God's hand was in it. So bold I was in my newfound faith that I hadn't stopped to think one minute what he might think about this statement. He smiled but took me seriously. He said, "I am not the owner here, my dad is, and he's in the office. Maybe I can get him to negotiate something."

The office was like walking into the 1970s. It had wood paneling, an old adding machine, phones with heavy receivers, and those old vinyl covered office chairs with little rips in them. I just smiled, knowing God was with me. The father came out. He had a kind face and grey hair, and I instantly knew he was a good man. I had to repeat the statement I had made earlier to his son. He also took me seriously, smiled, and said, "Well, here's what we can do. I'll come down to $2,500, and you can pay me the difference whenever you have the money. I won't charge you interest, and we'll keep the tally until the balance is paid off. I will let you take the car with the $1,500 you give me today." I smiled and knew I had just been given another gift from our Lord!

The car served me well; it was well worth what I paid for it. Every pay check I would go in and pay what I could to whittle the total down as quickly as possible. About two months after paying off the car, my younger sister Mae came to visit me. The car was having a problem with the break peddle. By chance, I happened to be driving right by the dealership on our way to the sledding hill with the boys. I drifted into a nearby parking lot and walked back to Shortie's. My sister was incredulous that I would ask them to help me, but she didn't understand the connection I had built with them. By this time, we had become real friends, sharing stories when I went in to make a payment. They had become like family to me. The son came out, hauled the car back to the dealership, gave us a loaner to go sledding, and fixed the problem for no charge while we were gone! What kind of used car dealership does that?! Only one that God had picked out for His child. I have asked God to bless those people and have sent people their way many times. That little car dealership is still in business after all these years, even in these hard times. God has blessed them. It is in giving we receive.

God used another situation to show me His love. We needed a couch for our living room. I didn't have any furniture, except the beds and the table, and the hutch in the kitchen. Still being in a self-absorbed faith, I asked the Lord for a couch like this. "Lord, I really could use a couch. A vanilla colored one with a floral print on it would be the one I would really like."

Later that week, there was a neighborhood rummage sale down the road from the apartment. I had never been to a rummage sale on my own, not since my own mother took us to them when I was a kid. But now, being in need, the idea was very attractive. Oh, how we change! One of the homes had grandparents moving in so they needed to get rid of many items, including a brand new vanilla colored couch — with a flower print! The man sold me the couch for $60 and even delivered it to my living room for me. I was beginning to see just how involved God was in the littlest details of my life. "Are not five sparrows sold for two pennies? And not one of them is forgotten before God. Why, even the hairs of your head are all numbered. Fear not; you are of more value than many sparrows" (Luke 12:6-7 RSVCE). I saw He really did love me. I saw this not because I got what I wanted, but because He cared enough about my wants.

Not until I was in trouble, called out to God, and learned that He was faithful did I start to trust in Him. I started to surrender and submit to His will. I saw that the suffering I had gone through, my enemies, so to speak, made me reach out in desperation. David long ago also learned this when he said, "Teach me Thy way, O LORD, and lead me on a level path because of my enemies" (Psalms 27:11 RSVCE).

My suffering had drawn me to reach out to Him as Savior. Jesus once asked the disciples, "But who do you say that I am?" Simon Peter replied, "You are the Christ, the Son of the living God."'" (Matthew 16:15-16, RSVCE). All names have an important meaning. Christ means "the anointed one" sent by God to save the world. From all that I had been through, God was asking me, "Who do you say that I am, Marie Therese?" I can now truly reply, "You are my Christ," not just for eternity, but right here in my daily life. He is my daily bread and refuge.

There is a verse in Isaiah that reminds me of this process in my life, my journey as it relates to joy and my struggles with power within and without. "The meek shall obtain fresh joy in the LORD, and the poor among men shall exult in the Holy One of Israel." (Isaiah29:19, RSVCE) I never realized meekness and joy go together. If we are meek then we show a mild humble quietness of nature; a healthy submissiveness that allows self not to demand its own will. It is a death to self ways so it lives in Christ's ways. Meekness was something foreign to me. Though I had been a shy, quiet girl when I was young, I always had a strong inner will that was not quiet. In most of my adult life, I did not want to be meek like Mary in the story with Martha, attentively listening for guidance at Jesus' feet. I hadn't learned that I needed to trust in Him, nor His guidance as the only safe journey with joy in it. Suffering had actually led me back to Jesus' level paths in meekness. I have learned through scriptures Peter 1:6-9 and Hebrews 12:13 that suffering leads to genuineness of faith, righteousness, joy, healing, and glory because it ultimately helps us die to self and desire God's will, which is the best way for us.

My power struggle with meekness blocked the path to joy in my journey. "Only step by step, and stage by stage, can you proceed, in your journey upward. The one thing to be sure of is that it is a journey with Me. There does come a Joy known to those who suffer with Me. But that is not the result of the suffering, but the result of the close intimacy with Me, to which suffering drove you" (*God Calling*, December 3, edited by AJ Russell). I had to fall to the bottom before I reached out to God. In return, He showered me with His love, provisions, and gifts and a relationship with Him, so that I would learn how much I was His child and that He had desired me my whole life. Jesus had been there my whole life as the suppliant, humbly begging, pleading for me to open myself to Him. He does not force His way in.

I had always seen our Majestic God as kind of a removed, lofty, tough guy, not a soft, loving, humble Savior with such loving eyes who would plead with me to be healed. "Draw nigh. Draw nigh, not as a suppliant, but as a listener. I am this Suppliant, as I make known to you My wishes. For this Majestic God is Brother, too, longing so intensely that you should serve your brother-man, and longing, even more intensely, that you should be true to that Vision He has of you" (*God Calling*, December 2, edited by AJ Russell). God wanted me to "be all I could be" as His child.

CHAPTER 5

"A Threefold Chord is not Quickly Broken" (Ecclesiastes 4:9-12 RSVCE)

Soon I began to get lonely. I had only been out on my own for a few months, but I had been separated longer from my husband in our home. Even before that I had not been intimate with my first husband for quite a long time, nor did I have really any close friendships. I longed for human touch, for conversation, for a man in my life with whom I could share memories and raise my boys. "Two are better than one because they have a good reward for their toil. For if they fall, one will lift up his fellow; but woe to him who is alone when he falls and has not another to lift him up. Again, if two lie together, they are warm; but how can one be warm alone? And though a man might prevail against one who is alone, two will withstand him. A threefold cord is not quickly broken" (Ecclesiastes 4:9-12 RSVCE). Yes, I wanted that human relationship. It is something we all strive for, regardless if we are called to marriage or being single. We need community and family. We were made to belong to God's family, for even the Holy Trinity is family, and we are made in God's image. It is no wonder why we need human touch, human love. It is a reflection of who He is.

So once again I went to prayer. "God, I know I am not worthy of another husband. I do not deserve it. I truly know it. But, You know my heart, You know what I need. I really would like a companion, a man in my life if You think it is the best thing. Please send me a good man."

At work, I was experimenting with annealing plastic parts, a process of heating up plastic back to its forming temperature to relax the form if it becomes warped in the cooling process. This experiment would save our company money on scrap if it worked out. The process required that I use a big walk-in oven in one of our company's big storage buildings. I didn't know it then, but we had an engineer there from Switzerland named Samuel who was training and experimenting on the same equipment with another worker, Joe. Joe's wife; Ellen, was a coworker of mine. We enjoyed talking with each other. She knew about my divorce and all it entailed and was looking out for me all the time. Their family was very involved in my life. Even their daughter was babysitting for me at my home. Joe and Ellen must have thought it would be good to get Samuel and I together because when I went over to the storage building to start annealing, Joe introduced me to Samuel. Right away I thought he was good looking but I really didn't think about God bringing someone to me at work. It never occurred to me. I figured God would bring him to me on my personal time. So I was pretty much clueless as to why Joe introduced us. I just went to work.

One of the quality men I was working with there was also a pilot. As we went about our work, we began to laugh and have a really good time talking about flying. Being alone that day, Samuel overheard our laughter and came over to see what the fun was about. We told him we were both pilots and explained our funny stories. He told us that he had been a jet crew chief for Swiss Air, had been in the military, and grew up on a farm! Soon we were all talking.

The next day Samuel came over and asked if I could talk with him. I said sure. Stepping away a bit, he asked if he could have my number. It was so cute for us both, me for not really knowing why he was getting my number and him because he was so nervous he had forgotten paper and had to write it on a piece of steal he had in his hand.

The next day he asked me to go out to dinner with him that evening. Still not getting the point about being asked on a date, I replied, "Oh, I

have bible study on Wednesday evenings. I'm sorry, but I can't miss it."
It wasn't until I talked to Ellen the next day that it really dawned on
me that Samuel had asked me out on a date. What was I thinking?! I
started to tear up, thinking, "I'm not sure if I'm dateable. I don't know
if I'm ready." In flooded the reality of my whole situation . . . dating
meant I was available, single, on my own.

After that I thought about Samuel, and decided that, yes, I really
did like him and even thought he was very good looking. He was six feet
tall with a good build and a nicely maintained goatee. He was a little
rugged and yet educated and refined at the same time, and he seemed
to be a good man. We were both into technical things, he graduated in
engineering and me mathematics, we both grew up on dairy farms, both
went into the army, and both had aviation backgrounds. Why hadn't
this all been obvious to me? I had even asked God about it. "Thank you,
God. And his name is even Samuel, which means; "God has heard"!
Wow, how did I miss this?"

Going back into work, I would go through the front on purpose
so I could walk by him, hoping to spur a conversation. Now that I was
interested, I guessed he'd read that I wasn't because he didn't ask me
out again but did continue to talk with me.

Soon the last day came for me to be in that building. I had to talk
with him or it would all be over. I asked God for a way to talk with
him. That day we happened to walk out to our cars alone at the same
time, so I said, "If you ever want to call me, or go out to dinner again,
I would like to." I was so nervous. Right away he got paper from his car
and asked me to write down my contact information.

He called me for a date that weekend. He had prepared a trip to
Detroit to the Ford auto museum. It sounded safe enough, but I assured
him I would not stay overnight there, that I had to be back home. He
wasn't sure how to date an American woman, and I wasn't sure what
he expected as a European. I had also decided not to let him meet my
boys until I was sure it would be serious.

The day went well. When we ate at the drive-through McDonald's
on the way, he let me pay. He thought American women felt it was rude
to be "taken care of," and he didn't want to offend me. Being poor I
had hoped for a nice meal on him. We still laugh about it today. Going

through the museum, every so often we brushed up against each other (maybe on purpose), and by the end of the day, we were holding hands. We talked all the way back and were both beginning to know this was special.

I remember wondering where he was staying and wanting to know more about him, how he was in his own environment. We had to drive by his hotel on the way to my apartment, so I asked if we could stop in and see his pictures of home. I really *did* want to know more about him though it may have sounded like something else. He understood that it was an apple not for picking, though the environment was tempting.

We walked up and he showed me pictures of home, friends, and his country. We were lying on our stomachs on the floor so that we could spread the pictures out. He gave me a kiss, and I returned it. It felt good, the touch, the being wanted. We kissed and then went a bit too far in our embrace but did not make love. He drove me home, and we both knew this was a start of something new.

On the next date, I decided to tell him my story about having been divorced twice and why. I didn't want him thinking I had kept anything from him, especially if it wasn't something he could live with. I wanted him to know I was transparent and honest; plus, I didn't want him to find out from anyone else but me. I knew that if God meant for it to be, he would somehow be ok with it, and if not, then it wasn't meant to be. "Do not lie to one another, seeing that you have put off the old nature with its practices and have put on the new nature, which is being renewed in knowledge after the image of its creator" (Colossians 3:9-10 RSVCE). "Deceit is in the heart of those who devise evil, but those who plan good have joy" (Proverbs 12:20 RSVCE). I had learned that God's way and will coupled with my meekness resulted in joy, so I had a strong conviction to tell the truth even if I knew it meant he might reject me.

My story didn't seem to bother him. He did say he would think it over, but that it probably wouldn't matter. I was relieved that all my past was known with nothing to hide. I had told him about my two young sons when we had talked before our first date. Now he knew everything about me. Odd thing is that he has told me, since he was a young man he always knew he would end up with a woman who had children that were not his, as if he had been mentally and spiritually prepared for it.

God does prepare us for what He brings us to. Samuel had never been married before and never had kids so how he accepted it all was even more impressive.

Since he knew my story, and things seemed to be getting more and more serious, I decided it was time to invite him over for a home-cooked meal to meet the boys. Billy was two years old and Raphael was now one and starting to walk. I dressed us all up for the event and made a good American meal with mashed potatoes, meat, and vegetables. I was so happy to see how he was with them — a good man with a good heart. The boys loved him. Again God was answering my prayers.

At some point early on, we discussed making love. I told him that to me it meant that we loved each other and had a commitment. I wasn't yet back into my Catholic faith, nor was I fully hearing what the Christian virtues taught to me by my Protestant bible study fully meant, but at least I finally realized that sex meant that you were seriously connected with someone. Somewhere in my conscience my mother was reminding me about chastity before marriage, but having still some relative truth, a nice apple, seemed convenient to my situation. I hadn't then realized why it wasn't healthy for me if I loved someone. The key to me was that I loved him. This kind of understanding would come with surrendering to more of His Way for me in obedience and Spiritual maturity.

Samuel, on the other hand, with his European background and not having frequented his Protestant church hadn't even considered that having sex before marriage was wrong. Even the concept of being serious with someone before sex was new to him. He took this new thought seriously though because he knew it was important to me. Also, he wasn't ready to say that he knew he loved me, which is what I told him the act of making love meant to me. So in the beginning of our relationship, we remained chaste. But the apple of it being ok before marriage was hanging there in front of our eyes.

Samuel was thirty-one, and I was thirty-three. We were both just getting over the desire to go out to the bars for entertainment. The old lifestyle of the twenties seemed to have slowly faded out of our lives. We started to investigate churches that we would enjoy going to together. He came with us to the nondenominational church I was attending, but it didn't seem right for us somehow. I had been doing bible studies with them since the retreat, and it had been very life giving, but one night, Pastor Brent came in to talk to our group. He started to speak about why Roman Catholic beliefs were dangerous for us, and I felt angry. The things he was saying didn't fit what I had learned growing up. I wanted to defend my old faith, even though I wasn't practicing it. Up until then, I had agreed with what I'd learned, and it had helped me, but this struck something deep in me. I remember the exact moment that evening when I knew I would not be returning to that church. I didn't have any bad feelings toward the people there. They had been instruments in God's hands to bring me back to my faith, but God had other plans for me.

I had a dream once that I believe was from God to illustrate such things in my life. I stood at the entrance of the banquet feast. My earthly father was with me, but I somehow knew he represented God the Father. In the entryway, there was a shelf with a sweet pastry that looked like a taco shell on it that I really wanted to eat, but it was too high for me to reach. I asked the Father again and again for it. He didn't say no, but gently and patiently kept trying to tell me that He had so much more in store for me. I couldn't seem to understand Him and kept asking for the pastry. So calmly, lovingly, He reached for the pastry and handed it to me. Then He led me out of the entrance into the banquet hall. It was a very large room without finite walls. In the middle, was a huge table, irregular in shape that faded into the distance. At the front of the table was a large chocolate cross (I really love chocolate) and all around it were plates and plates of the most delicious food I had ever seen in my life. My family was seated all around the table happily talking with each other. None of them were eating. They didn't seem to need to. It was as if the food was part of their joy in just being there.

Since then I have come to realize that the food was the fruits of the Spirit like the ones described in Galatians. "But the fruit of the Spirit is love, joy, peace, patience, kindness, goodness, faithfulness, gentleness, self-control; against such there is no law. And those who belong to Christ Jesus have crucified the flesh with its passions and desires."(Galations5:22-23, RSVCE) These were the rungs of the ladder in my previous dream, the ones that Mary Agreda talked about being virtues that I needed to learn so I could sing in joy to heaven. He didn't want me to keep reaching for better. No, as His child He wanted me to have the best way, His way.

God the Father seemed to be showing me, and still is, that through Jesus and the Holy Spirit I could have so much more than what I was asking for. He wasn't telling me it was bad for me to go to the church I'd been going to, but like the pastry, I would not be getting all that He had planned for me if I stayed there.

So Samuel and I started shopping for churches. Some were big band performances. The music was fun, but it left me wanting more . . . more that didn't come, even when the pastor spoke. People there would look for new faces and while you were listening and clapping to the drumbeat, they were busy taking the number off the back of your seat and sending it off to their evangelists. The numbers were so that all the evangelizers could locate where you were and be standing by your aisle to make sure you didn't leave without being spoken to again.

After the last of the music played, they cornered us, ushered us into one of their private rooms, evangelized us, gave us pamphlets, and asked for our contact information. It all felt very pushy and smothering. It was way over the top for Samuel who was coming from a conservative area in Switzerland where their faith was traditionally quiet and mostly a private thing.

We tried others here and there, but none seemed to fit his conservative background or my Catholic whisperings. It slowly dawned on me to try the local Catholic Church. It was an instant fit. Who would have thought it?

We continued to frequent the Catholic Church that was half way between our homes. It was a parish in the country with guitar and organ music. I started to remember what the other churches were lacking — Jesus' real presence and His sacrifice and resurrection in the Eucharist; His principle channel to communicate His gift of grace is given to us in this sacrament that the other churches were lacking. "So Jesus said to them, 'Truly, truly, I say to you, unless you eat the flesh of the Son of man and drink his blood, you have no life in you; he who eats my flesh and drinks my blood has eternal life, and I will raise him up at the last day. For my flesh is food indeed, and my blood is drink indeed. He who eats my flesh and drinks my blood abides in me, and I in him. As the living Father sent me, and I live because of the Father, so he who eats me will live because of me'" (John 6:53-57 RSVCE).

I sensed this timelessness in God and His Presence and grace available at mass in my inner being, though it would take another five years before I fully believed that the Eucharist was truly Him. There were blocks such as selfishness, immaturity, and even some unforgiveness that still kept me from all God had meant for me.

The word Eucharist in the Catholic mass refers to the holy sacrifice of Jesus and our own "yes" to the sacrifice of self mingled with His. His sacrifice gives us the grace to overcome our selfish desires so we can be holy like Him, we can't do it without His grace. Once years later when I was at daily mass during the Liturgy of the Eucharist I saw our priest in a vision hold up the consecrated host of Jesus and break it in half. When he did this I saw a color close to blue and grey of particles mixed with light which broke out over all of the people there. When I was home a few days later I was cleaning up and found an old holy card of the Divine Mercy of God from Sister Faustina. God was helping me understand His gifted vision.

Sister Faustina was given a vision of Jesus' pierced side from the cross and from it was flowing a blue and greyish light along with red light next to it. She was given this explanation from God, "The two rays denote Blood and Water. The pale ray stands for the Water which makes souls righteous. The red ray stands for the Blood which is the life of souls. These two rays issued forth from the very depths of My tender mercy when My agonized heart was opened by a lance on the Cross. These rays shield souls from the wrath of My Father. Happy is the one who dwell in their shelter, for the just hand of God shall not lay hold of him." (Diary of Saint Maria Faustina Kowalski; entry299) Sister Faustina was given the words, "Jesus I trust in You," along with this vision. Jesus wanted me to see visibly that His mercy and grace were bigger than my past sins or future struggles. He wanted me to know; the more I trusted in Him the more grace I would be open to receive. His grace and mercy in my vision at church that day showed me that they flow from His holy sacrifice in and through His sacraments in His holy church. That He was indeed there, His side was pierced on the cross and His grace was flowing through the Eucharist out onto us all. In my life

I needed to trust in Jesus's sacrifice for me fully by being in His graces of the Sacraments of His holy church. I needed to go to confession, and then to receive Him fully surrendered to Him in trust.

One of the spiritual fruits is loving our Eucharistic Lord. It is a celebration of our unity and communion with Him. I needed to die to self in a real way, not just physically, but spiritually and morally to be more like Him, more in union with Him. As Father John A. Hardon said in the *S. J. Archives: Sacrifice Sacrament of the Holy Eucharist*; "We will benefit only as much from the graces of the sacrament sacrifice of the Mass as we mirror the image of the life of Christ in our lives." I was still in the baby stages of my walk, still having a faith that was centered on me. God wanted me to move on from spiritual milk to other foods. He also wanted me to know what I was receiving and the status of my own soul before doing so. "Whoever, therefore, eats the bread or drinks the cup of the Lord in an unworthy manner will be guilty of profaning the body and blood of the Lord. Let a man examine himself, and so eat of the bread and drink of the cup. For anyone who eats and drinks without discerning the body eats and drinks judgment upon himself. That is why many of you are weak and ill, and some have died. But if we judged ourselves truly, we should not be judged" (1 Corinthians 11:27-31 RSVCE).

I have come to learn the following through the rosary's fifth luminous mystery: Institution of the Eucharist, and its reflections(Praying the Rosary Without Distractions ©1994, 2010, Dominican Fathers) given for the eighth through the tenth beads:

8. The Eucharist is a sacrifice inasmuch as it is offered up, and a sacrament inasmuch as it is received.
9. In the Mass we offer ourselves to God, and God gives himself to us.
10. The Mass will be fruitful in the measure of our surrender to the Father.

Since I hadn't fully surrendered my selfish ways before receiving His Holy Sacrament, I couldn't embrace my own sacrifice nor fully understand Jesus' sacrifice for me thereby uniting the two as an offering when I received the Eucharist. The Lord was showing me this gently, leading and guiding me to a more unselfish faith and an ability to receive a more fullness of His grace waiting for me.

Since the morning before the retreat, I got up at 3:30 am everyday to read the Bible and spend valuable time with God before work. I started to journal all that I was being shown so that I could go back and read it and know that I had grown from one day, month, and year to the next. Those times with God in the privacy of the dark morning hours gave me the grace to handle the long hard hours and receive what God was trying to show me. He gave me little messages that invariably matched a problem I was facing to help me through it.

One of these mornings, I felt a strong desire to own a home again. I knew it was like asking for a man in my life, something I didn't really deserve after my history. But where did the desire come from? I tested it out, and it didn't seem to be coming just out of selfish wants. It just seemed silly to throw money away on rent when I could be putting it into a home.

The desire did not go away. Knowing I had gone into bankruptcy over the last two homes, I figured I'd be out of luck, but my track record with prayer was awesome, so I kept praying. I got in touch with a realtor and asked her what she could do. She told me I didn't have a chance at a mortgage, but she would look into it anyway and give me a call. I kept praying. Her call back was not promising, but she said she had a contact that may be able to help me out and to give him a call.

When I called him, it turned out that he had served as a captain in the active duty army. He had gotten out and was now a mortgage broker. He said he would work with me, but that I would have to write a letter to a judge explaining my situation and why I had had foreclosures in the past. When I wrote this, I didn't blame anyone, but stated the case, the affair, the divorces, the abuse, and the whole messy thing up to how we had had to go bankrupt. I really didn't expect the judge to have mercy on me given that the bankruptcy had been part of the affair, but after only a few weeks, it came back approved for up to $100,000. I was ecstatic. This was another God gift that I didn't deserve. God was trusting me, so I had to trust Him. I was not going to let Him down!

I knew I probably couldn't find a home under $100,000 suitable for us, but God was at work.

I looked and looked and looked. It wasn't as easy as I thought it would be. I looked at double wides, broken down homes, old farm houses too big to heat, houses in bad neighborhoods — nothing seemed to be coming up. Samuel came with us to look at many of them, but he didn't like most of them either. Samuel had to fly back to Europe for a few weeks, so I kept looking during that time. I found a home in a town called Greenville that was much like the one I grew up in; in the country with a river running through it. It was 41 miles away from work, but after all that looking, I was ready to go for it. I loved that old farmhouse. It came with five acres and a big garage. It was being sold by a couple who were divorcing. They had started remodeling it but hadn't finished. There were some problems with the house. It was old and still had old newspaper for insulation. It had a Michigan basement, which means that part of the floor was cement, the other part dirt, and the outside needed siding. They wanted to sell it for $65,000. My mortgage would allow me to take the whole $100,000 and put the difference into fixing the home.

I decided it would work, but I should have asked God and Samuel first. You would think by this time I would have understood that His guidance was best. But instead I thought I had the green light all the way. I signed for the home with a contract that stated I would have to pay $2,000 if I wanted to back out. I wasn't worried about this since I thought I had finally found the one I wanted.

I called Samuel that night and told him about the house. He was skeptical but excited to see it. When he got back, we went to look at the home, and he instantly said he would pay for me to get out of the contract. He explained that the drive would be costly and driving after overtime would be dangerous. He said that it would be too far for him to easily come visit, and he reminded me of the need for immediate reaction time to daycare calls. Then he pointed out the obvious care that the house would need and the time it would require from me that I didn't have. All of these were correct, but I really wrestled with giving up what I really wanted verses what was better for the whole; for Samuel, for the kids. I loved the nostalgia of the house and had acted on feelings.

God had brought Samuel into my life to help me be more even keeled and to see things I didn't. He gave me a kind of guide in him. Despite this, I felt angry and frustrated and had lots of justification for why I did what I did. But in the end, after much prayer and many tears, I told Samuel I would allow him to back me out of the contract and go back to the searching. I believe this was kind of a test to help me learn how to give up self for others. It was also a way for me to see how God guides us like a father, or husband should, and where we need to surrender to healthy guidance. He was showing me the difference between control I'd known and the guidance that was a gift available always through obedience to His holy way.

I was learning to be open to Jesus talking to me in and through His people. I had not known a man in my life other than my earthly father who I could trust to give me really good personal guidance. Because of the choices I had made with my two ex-husbands, trusting and discerning Samuel's guidance was hard for me. Now I had to accept and surrender to sharing power and decision-making and trust and that Samuel really wanted the best for us, not just himself. I was learning how to be part of a couple who helped each other out for the good of the partnership not just for the good of the individuals. I asked myself, "Can I really trust him? Will he stick around long enough to experience whatever home I choose?" My answer was strongly, "Yes, I know God brought him into my life. I know God will watch over us. He is helping me with Samuel's guidance. I have to listen to Him through Samuel." It was an excellent introduction to what God's bigger family was supposed to do for each other.

But giving up being in charge of all decisions came long and hard for me, especially because of my background with abusive control and my own military authority as a commander. This surrender was a power struggle inside me, but in the end I had come to realize Jesus' love for me was faithful, trustworthy and something I desperately needed to keep clinging to.

A few weeks went by, and I saw another home in the paper that I had seen before but had skimmed over. It kept coming back to me. I finally decided to drive out and look at it, and as soon as I saw it, I loved it! This time I decided to pray and then get the realtor and Samuel to go with me to look inside. It was a two-story brick home in good condition a wonderful one-acre yard up on a hill one mile from a small town called Restore (among the best 100 small towns in the nation), only twenty miles from work — and it was within my price range. It was on Hole Four of the neighborhood golf course and had very nice, older neighbors. It came with a washer, dryer, and appliances...this was the banquet house...not the little pastry on the shelf! I couldn't believe it. I had almost missed it!

Those years on Hammond Road in Restore were some of the sweetest, most memorable years of my life. They were healing, restful times in which I bonded with my boys and felt accepted and loved by my community. Samuel was there right along with us to celebrate those blessings he had been part of guiding us to. We started a garden and worked on beautifying the home. I enrolled the kids on the town soccer team. The local Catholic Church had a wonderful small school, and after praying about the cost, I decided to enroll Billy there for kindergarten. Both neighbors were like grandparents for us . . . we had family! Jerry, the older man who lived on the left of us, would take the boys out for rides on his golf cart. They just loved him. Whenever the kids went over to their home, Elaine, his wife, would always be there with a candy bowl ready. They even babysat when Samuel and I went out for a date. On the right lived Molly, a woman in her eighties, who had a dog that the kids really loved. The dog's name was Sam, a bit controversial with Samuel having the same name, but funny nonetheless. We went for walks with Molly every Wednesday after I got home from work. There was a small sheep farm across the road owned by a sister to the man who lived three homes down from me. Both of his sons lived two doors down on either side of us. Whenever I had trouble with a lawn mower or anything, they would come over to help without me even asking, like the time I put the blades on upside down on my riding lawn mower after having them sharpened. Yes, we had family, and we were starting to belong. God was strengthening in me the belief that I could trust in His bigger family and their guidance. What blessings come from obedience to Christ and His ways!

CHAPTER 6

"Led Back to the Unity from Which We Were Fragmented" – St. Augustine

Back in 2000, there was a bit of a slump in our state's economy that affected the company I worked for. We had troubles with furniture sales; our company was not only a supplier to the auto industry, but we also made office chairs. Because the sales were down on the chairs, our company had to cut back. That meant people were being moved around the company, and managers, like myself, were concerned that they may have to look for a new job. I was a first shift supervisor with low seniority, so they asked me to go to second shift. This was hard for me as a single mother, but luckily the boys were one year away from all day school, so I had a bit of time to get myself back on the first shift if need be. In the meantime, I started to pray about what God wanted me to do and started searching for another first shift position outside of the company.

I found an ad in the newspaper that was simply unbelievable. It read something like this: "Needed: Project Manager, four year college mathematics degree required. Must have manufacturing management background, military helicopter avionics knowledge, preferably military officer experience, and some sense of European culture." I just stared at this ad. "Are you kidding?" I said out loud. It was as if someone had made this job for me. And the timing! I immediately sent in my resume and was called in for an interview. The fit was perfect and they offered me the job on the spot. It paid more than double than I was making, which would even be enough to hire a nanny if I needed one. But there was a big glitch . . . this apple was so shiny that I didn't see the big worm at first . . . or didn't *want* to see it. The job entailed being a liaison between this company and the military and required that I be on the road about ten days or more a month going to air shows in California, Wisconsin (which was even more of a temptation being close to my parents farm), and places in Europe, like the Paris Air show. The time away would mean the boys would either be left with a nanny or have to go to their dad's. Neither one seemed to be a good choice for the kids, maybe for me if I were alone, but not for our little family, and I knew it. Ten days out of the working month meant almost half the time. I couldn't do that to us no matter what the price was. "Lord, what is this?" I asked. I went home full of mixed emotions. I cried, rationalized some, prayed, and by the time I was nearing home, I was leaning toward calling the company back and telling them I couldn't take the job.

My options were to take this job and be gone half the time or be on second shift and be rung out from the hours. Being on second shift management meant going in around 3:00 pm and get out around 1:00 am. By the time I would get home and let the sitter go, it would be around 2:00 am. I was worried about how hard it would be to find anyone willing to watch the kids at those hours. With the kids getting up around 6:30 am this schedule would leave me around four hours of sleep a night.

Now it was time to pray and trust. I had been given options, but they didn't seem like options. God was telling me to take the second shift, I knew it, but it didn't seem like I would be able to endure it. It was a test in giving outside of what was good for the self alone and to help me learn to trust that the Lord would provide. "The sun shall not smite you by day, nor the moon by night. The Lord will keep you from all evil; He will keep your life. The Lord will keep your going out and your coming in from this time forth and for evermore" (Psalms 121:6-8 RSVCE).

Second shift did not seem like God was giving me His best provisions, but I had learned that He was faithful. Sometimes the Lord's provision for us is not exactly how we imagine it should be. Elijah, whose name means "Yahweh is my God," was God's holy prophet. He also had such provisions given to him in 1Kings12-17. He was on the run from King Ahab during a drought. There he was, one of God's most powerful witnesses, on the run, and the provision God sent him were ravens and a poor, dying widow. He provided Elijah with shelter, water, and food though it was not on a tablecloth in a rich environment, but in humble circumstances that would lead to more growth for him and for others who were also suffering.

Like Elijah, I was in trouble and wanting to do His will. Second shift looked as if it was ravens or starving widows feeding me in a drought, and yet I was thankful for the provision, for after all it was a provision in my own kind of drought. So, according to God's word, I, too, followed my Savior's promptings for His safe provision, not fully knowing how it would turn out.

I had to interview sitters to come into my home to take care of the kids so they could sleep in their own beds. Finally, I narrowed it down and hired a person I felt I could trust, though this too was a bit like the raven story in that she was tough on our family. When I found she did not live by faith, I tried to show her how it had changed my life. She told me she was married to a man who was in jail for theft and had a small son who would need to come with her. After much prayer I felt as though God was telling me to give her a chance. She needed the job and was good with the kids . . . or so I thought.

Second shift went as I assumed it would, and it only lasted one year. With only four hours of sleep a night, I was exhausted. But to my surprise, I also found joy and rebuilding. I decided to make that situation glorify God. I knew He had sent me there, so I also knew He would be with me. At the time, the second shift was known as the worst shift: messy and nonproductive with the what everyone believed were the largest scrap rates. They were the misfits.

I got the group together, and we decided right from the beginning that we would be blameless for God. One of the men had been a drug addict but had recently surrendered to God's way. He desperately wanted to turn his personal life around and his work life, too. He actually had the word "blameless" marked in his bible and showed it to us. Another man was a poor immigrant who'd gotten his citizenship but was separated from his family, struggling to stay afloat and send money back home. Another was a young woman who had a child with a man she wasn't married to and was living in poor conditions. We all had stories, but God had brought us together in our lowliness to work together for something better, for hope, for unity. Not all the second shifters were active Christians, but they were ready for a change, for hope of a better reputation, for someone to believe in them. And there I was among them, like Elijah with the ravens and the dying widow. "Do all things without grumbling or questioning that you may be blameless and innocent, children of God without blemish in the midst of a crooked and perverse generation, among whom you shine as lights in the world, holding fast the word of life" (Philippians 2:14-16 RSVCE). We wanted to shine like stars in spite of our darkness, and maybe because of it. "Blameless" became our new shift motto. I spoke to them about faith, how God was with us, and how I expected great things to come from that shift.

Despite how it might appear to others, we decided to track our scrap. No other shift posted this. We had the place shiny and clean for the third shift, and soon people started to take notice. The first shift supervisor liked the clean area, but he didn't like the reports on the board. Soon he started to have problems on his shift with his personnel. Our reports started to beg the question what were the actual scrap rates of the first and third shift. In fact, could they quantitatively show they were better than everyone else like they'd been saying? First shift people started to argue. Their safety record went down as accidents started to happen. They blamed each other for the problems, and their morale started to drop. By tracking our mistakes truthfully and publically, no one could blame us for what was not true, though they tried. This put a mirror of responsibility on them that they were not ready for.

If we start doing God's will, we must expect that evil will come in with a vengeance to stop the truth from spreading. When this happens, we can't let it frighten us into stopping doing His will. We must endure with courage. "First realize very fully that when you have heard My voice and are going to fulfill your mission to work for Me and to draw souls to Me, you must expect a mighty onslaught from the evil one who will endeavor with all his might to frustrate you and to prevent your good work. Expect that" (*God Calling Devotional* 12/6). The people on our shift started to take more responsibility for changeovers, scrap rates, and cleanliness. We did not blame each other but stuck together accepting responsibility of the whole both individually and as a group. Now we saw that we needed to unify all the shifts and get them to see that what we were doing would be a good thing for the whole of the plant, not just for shifts to battle against each other.

People on our shift had become a cohesive family. We even read a verse here and there together. As we became as blameless as possible for God, our scrap and production rates became the best in the whole plant. The plant manager saw all this and asked me to take over the whole operation and come back onto first shift. Soon I had, or rather all of us working with God, had the whole plant running smoothly, so smoothly that it seemed I had worked myself right out of a job. Sure there were glitches here and there and some days were hard, but on the whole, we were going in the right direction. The people ran the plant without needing help. They could order supplies, ship out the product, change over the machine from part number to the next within record time, and even do minor repairs without any help. They felt empowered, unified, and took ownership for what was going out. This was a far cry from what it was when I came, but it didn't come without rebellion from some. God meant for me to be on that shift to motivate others to His call and to give Him glory. Even though it didn't look like excellent provision, it was!

I was learning as a leader that working for the betterment of the whole was actually better for me in the long run. Hiding mistakes and keeping secrets was a slow death. I realized that leadership was a gift given in His provision and for His glory. I learned in retrospect it mirrors the marriage relationship with God and with earthly spouses. The more we use the gift of leadership in Truth for the betterment of the whole, the more the whole is healthy and productive. Leading in God's power and way was much more rewarding, exciting, and challenging!

Though things were going great at work, back at home, we started to have trouble with the sitter being rough on the boys. For example, she would not allow them to come in from outside when they wanted, and she was gruff with them when they didn't eat all their food. She turned up the thermostat to her liking, which caused high bills and even caused problems with my old furnace. I found frogs in my bed and other strange things. One day, I found the bible I had given her for Christmas in the back of our upstairs hall closet. I really tried with her, but in the end I had to let her go.

I believe that time was for her more than for us. It didn't hurt us. It only gave us challenges, but I know after our time she must have at least questioned her faith and saw that God loved her. We had reached out to her; we even went to her home. She ate supper at our table every night. Sometimes we just don't get to see the whys, but the answers are there. In her place we found the most wonderful daycare lady I could have ever wished for! She was a miracle. We kept her the rest of the time, and the boys actually asked to go to her home to play on weekends! We still exchange Christmas cards after eight years. God's reprieve came through just when we needed it.

Samuel and I dated for four-and-a-half years from April 1999 to October 2003. After the first few dates and discussing what making love meant to us, that apple seemed to be looming over us more and more as we became serious in our relationship. It was harder on the weekends when the kids went to their dad's, leaving us home alone. The door seemed to fly open and justifications rushed in as soon as we told each other that we loved one another. Didn't that mean that we wanted to surrender to each other totally?

Samuel's European background lent a liberal view on premarital sex and sex in general. He had learned that sex was normal way of experiencing someone, even on the first date. To him it wasn't a matter of a moral sin at all. He justified that we had to see if the physical worked with us. Wasn't that important to know so that it was one less thing to worry about for a marriage someday? It seemed like a good argument but my past experiences, the old conscience, and my mother's warnings from my teens came flooding in. Why did it bother me? Why did I feel so guilty about making love with him if I loved him? I definitely knew

I did not want him to move in with me if we were not married, but why should that be any different than making love with him? I justified the difference solely because of the children. Living together was showing the children a wrong lifestyle, especially if the relationship didn't turn out after they had gotten used to him as a father figure. But making love with him without their knowing it did not hurt them or me — or so I thought. I had one foot in hot water and one out.

I struggled with what my desires wanted and what my conscience was telling me. God was leading me to purity so that I would be able to have a clear mind and wisdom to make sound judgments, but the self battled with temptations and justifications. "The chaste person maintains the integrity of the powers of life and love placed in him. This integrity ensures the unity of the person and is opposed to any behavior that would impair it. It tolerates neither a double life nor duplicity in speech."(CCC 2338). Here is that duplicity of mind and soul that St. Augustine talks about: "Indeed it is through chastity that we are gathered together and led back to the unity from which we were fragmented into multiplicity" (CCC 2340; Jacques-Paul Migne, *Patrologia Latina*, V. 32: 796). As stated in Galatians 15:22, chastity is a moral virtue and also a gift from God, a kind of grace, a fruit of spiritual effort. My conscience and the world were telling me two different things. I was reeling inside, waiting for a decision. It left me frustrated and guilty. The question I had to answer was, "Why did I think living together without marriage was a wrong lifestyle to show the kids?" This question would then answer the question of sex before marriage. I realized that it came down to a level of commitment. When you give yourself fully to someone, it should be fully, not partially, which gives a way out. If we lived together, I would be saying to Samuel, "You are in a trial period, and I do not want to commit to you fully right now." Having sex before marriage is no different, for it says, "I want to experience you physically without commitment." In both cases, there is a lack of full giving but a desire to have full pleasure.

Some may ask, "How do you know if you are sexually compatible if you don't live together or have sex before marriage?" For me, the more we got to know each other, the more I realized that the love I had for Samuel was not based on feelings that come and go like the wind or from temporary physical pleasure, but from actions of free will. This came out of knowing who he was. We were helping each other grow toward holiness, making each other the people we were meant to be. It says in the CCC; "The vocation to marriage is written in the very nature of man and woman as they came from the hand of the Creator." (CCC1603) We are called to marriage as a vocation, just like single or consecrated life. Some of us, like me, need marriage to learn more of salvation and grow in holiness. If holiness is established as a goal first, then the other will flow as we fully commit to each other out of respect for the other person's integrity. If it happens the other way, we are left with less respect for the integrity of our partner, our union or ourselves. Problems grow so subtly out of this lack of respect and self-control. "Chastity includes an *apprenticeship in self-mastery* which is a training in human freedom. The alternative is clear: either man governs his passions and finds peace, or he lets himself be dominated by them and becomes unhappy.(CF. Sirach1:22) 'Man's dignity therefore requires him to act of conscious and free choice, as moved and drawn in a personal way from within, and not by blind impulses in himself or by mere external constraint. Man gains such dignity when, ridding himself of all slavery to the passions, he presses forward to his goal by freely choosing what is good and, by his diligence and skill, effectively secures for himself the means suited to this end.'(GS17)" (CCC 2339).

Making choices out of free will instead of enslavement to temporary physical desire led us to a freedom in our relationship because we governed our passions instead of our passions governing us. We needed to be free to love the person without the enslavement of seeing the other as an object of our physical desires, especially before the marriage decision, so that we were clear in mind in the choice we were making for each other. But we had to go through a learning stage of all this first to see it clearly.

There were a few rough areas we dealt with after having sex before marriage. Without the commitment, it seemed there was a lack of sincerity, holiness, and integrity toward one another. Somehow finding out more about the spiritual and mental part of our relationship seemed to lessen as the physical took more precedence. It nearly caused us to separate once.

A casual sex partner from Samuel's past named Isla came back into his life for a week. He told me that back then they'd planned and paid for a trip to Bali together and that the time had come for them to go. He assured me that now they were only friends, that she knew about me, and the trip would be harmless. He asked me if I minded if he still went. Naively trusting him, I replied, "As long as it's just friends, I guess I don't see a problem." I sounded like Jason so long ago, though deep inside, I really didn't want him to go. So he spent the week with her, took her shopping with him to buy things for the boys, and told her all about me. After they got back, Samuel had to go back to Europe for a week or so. One night I called, and she was there with him. He told me she needed a place to sleep for the night on her way back to England. I started to feel that it wasn't just a platonic relationship but a physical one. I guess I really hadn't wanted the inner feeling and truth to be confirmed, not after my past, but it was as I thought — they were indeed sleeping together. He thought this to be an inconsequential time, but it meant everything to me. It left me feeling less than important, no different than any other girl he'd ever met. Though the devil may have meant it for bad, God would use it for good. "But Joseph said to them, 'Fear not, for am I in the place of God? As for you, you meant evil against me, but God meant it for good, to bring it about that many people should be kept alive, as they are today.'"(Ge50:19-20 RSVCE) It helped us to see that we were playing with fire.

Samuel's involvement with Isla was an eye opener. After Bali, she wrote him letters and even addressed one to me, making me feel like the other woman. I considered stopping our relationship because of his involvement with her, but because he really loved me and cared about our relationship's future, he took a first time serious look at his sexual choices. Now he was facing the reality of what that meant. We both began to see that our commitment and our sexual activity were not rightly aligned. It took time, and God was patient with us, but slowly we saw His plan and intentions for us.

About the same time this happened, we started to look for a church together that I mentioned earlier. We were both seeking, searching for holiness and real answers in our lives. Samuel was tired of the old way, the "free self life," and so was I. Along with consistently going to church with us every week, he was starting to look deeper into his own moral and spiritual life, as was I.

When I told him how his involvement with Isla hurt me and that I thought we should call it off, he began to realize just how important we were to him. He was going to lose what he loved because he hadn't really realized or discerned that his choices and their consequences affected others. This whole thing with Isla also opened our eyes to our pasts. I wanted to forgive, wanted to know that this truly was love I was feeling with him. I realized that Samuel really did love me when I saw the hurt in his eyes in response to my own hurt. We needed to realize the sin, forgive each other and ourselves, and move on. As slowly as we could handle it, God had shown us our sin without leaving us in despair. This helped us discern that we were meant for each other. Samuel wanted to get married, but I needed more time. We started going to mass every weekend, praying together, and desiring more and more of what God wanted. We fell deeply in love and found an inner intimacy we hadn't had before.

I remember when it hit Samuel that I was the one. We were sitting on a dock in Niagara Falls talking about his brother who had passed away seven years earlier, talking about our lives, faith, and who we were. Later when we were driving, he pulled over at a rest stop and shouted joyfully out the window and gave me a big hug. At that moment, he realized I loved him in spite of his mistakes. I loved him for who he was; he had never been loved like that before. He looked at me and loved me deeply for who I was, for my faith, and for my desire for holiness. He wanted to be with me and share it all together.

During that time, Samuel would come out to our home and help us with yard work and fixing up the place. He helped us dig out all the metal fence posts set in concrete around the whole yard, we put an ad in the paper, and sold the fence for a much needed $800. I was amazed. He put in drainage pipes on the side of the house so the basement would dry up, and it worked wonderfully! He made a beautiful wooden flagpole for me, one that could come down with a hinge. We planted shrubs and a nice big garden. The first Christmas he secretly found a used Simplicity Wisconsin riding lawn mower on sale in town with snow blower and had it hiding in the back shed for Christmas morning. That mower was the best tangible gift I had ever received. It saved many backbreaking hours of manually pushing the mower up the hill or shoveling snow. He built shelves for the basement and built stands for the washer and dryer. We even cut out a wall in the kitchen to open up the room and had the cut on the ceiling finished off. I received a discarded heavy industrial skid from work that two of my coworkers delivered for me to use as a base for the kids' playhouse and swing set. Samuel helped me put it all together and even built an upstairs platform, like a rock climbing surface that led to a fort. The house was becoming our home.

Sam had always had a desire to go sailing. Since we had both been raised on a farm, neither of us knew the first thing about it. He started pricing sailboats, and soon he found an old 1976 twenty-seven foot Catalina. Lake Huron had low water levels that year and many of the sailors with over four feet of draft had their boats up on cradles with "For Sale" signs on them. This was the case for the one he'd found. He had it shipped over to Lake Michigan where we had found a nice affordable little marina. Because of God's forgiveness and all that He had brought us through, we named the boat Second Chances. We changed the stripping color and the wording to green meaning of hope and new life.

We learned so much about ourselves on that sailboat together. Though we had many disagreements and discussions, my first lesson was allowing Samuel to be captain of the vessel and learning to be comfortable in the role of support. His lesson as an engineer and intellectual was how to trust in his crew. I was used to being in charge, calling the shots, and being at the helm, even when the burden was too heavy for me. On a sailboat, just like in the military, the crew needs to know who the captain is, and the captain needs to know he can rely on the crew, especially in rough waters or precarious situations like running aground, motor failure, or a sick captain. I learned there was indeed power in the support role and that the captain needed me to be "all that I could be" or the sailing wouldn't be as smooth or in some cases even possible. I was learning I could be powerful and useful without being the one in charge or in the limelight. Over time this concept has been liberating, relieving me of a burden I didn't need to carry. It was one of my first opportunities to embrace meekness that would eventually help me find joy in the journey. "The meek also shall obtain fresh joy in the LORD" (Isaiah 29:19 RSVCE).

Once when we were still really new to sailing, our atomic four engine stopped running because of some sludge that had floated back into the tank, so we had to sail it back in without a motor at the mercy of the wind. Samuel let me take the helm while he worked the sails, and we sailed it right into our slip like a couple of old salts.

We learned how to live and work together without the possibility of running away when we got frustrated. The boys also had to learn how to get along in small confines. There were those windy, sunny, beautiful days of fast sails and anchored near sandy harbors swimming off the bow. There were days where we just wanted to sell the boat, but it always called us back to the closeness it had helped foster. We also met the most wonderful man, Scott Daniels, a single man in his early fifties, who was our dock mate and also had a sailboat. He became part of our family over time. Through the years, Second Chances helped us make the transition to more mature, intimate union and family living. We see it as grace from our loving God.

During the time of Second Chances and the Restore house we found out that out our company could not renew Samuel's visa and that he'd have to go back full time to Europe. Trying to be obedient to whatever God was showing us, we decided to end our romantic relationship and just be friends. We were afraid that the long distance relationship would not work and that it must have been God's will for us to end it. Who were we kidding?! We learned that sometimes our discernment of God's guidance in difficulties is askew. God had brought us together, and He was showing us strongly again to trust in Him even if it looked impossible. That would be cemented in after a more difficult learning curve. And so we went on bravely trying to be "just friends."

We were both invited to a wedding several months before he was to go. My youngest was the ring bearer. It was strange to not go together, strange to see him talking with others without me, not to sit with me, and to act almost as if I was not there. I expected him to talk with me like we used to, come over by me, maybe even dance with me . . . but he didn't, and it bothered me. Even the mother of the bride said to me, "Did you see how Sam is talking with those people and not spending time with you? Doesn't it make you feel bad?" It seemed there was always someone pointing out the obvious to me right where it hurt the most. I just wanted to run from the wedding. I think he was protecting his own feelings, but I couldn't take it any longer. It was about 10:00 pm and thought I'd waited long enough to leave to be appropriate. I decided to go without saying goodbye to him, wanting to just leave the sorrow behind without being noticed. I was embarrassed that my feelings for him were so deep though he didn't seem to be having any trouble.

With tears running down my face, I got the kids in the car and started to drive out of the parking lot, saying "Lord help me! I can't do this on my own. It hurts too much. Please help me to understand Your will." Samuel must have been watching me without my knowing it and realized I was missing. As I was driving up to the road from the parking lot, he came running toward the car.

"Stop! I didn't get to say goodbye. Why are you leaving so soon?"

"I just can't pretend not to care," I explained. "I can't pretend that the feelings are not there. My heart is breaking, and I can't stay any more. It hurts too much." He said he was going through the same hurt as me but was trying to respect our decision and that he would call me. I drove home in tears, trying not to alarm the kids, but feeling a welling up of deep sorrow.

After we talked, we got back together because we did love each other, but we still didn't know what to do about the visa. We didn't want to marry just so he could stay. That was too much pressure. We decided to pray about it together, something we should have done first. "Again I say to you, if two of you agree on earth about anything they ask, it will be done for them by My Father in heaven. For where two or three are gathered in My name, there am I in the midst of them" (Matthew 18:19-20 RSVCE). I remember praying together on the shores of Lake Michigan on the dunes. We decided to give all our future to God, whatever He decided to do. We told Him we loved each other, wanted the past to be forgiven, and would honor Him in His decision, and we both meant it. Saying goodbye to Samuel at the airport with the boys was very difficult. It was a visual of really surrendering to God's will that I will never forget. I wasn't sure if I'd ever see him again, wasn't sure if it was our last goodbye. He hugged the boys goodbye, then me with tears in his eyes, and he was off with a wave of his hat. I didn't let the tears show until he was walking away toward his airplane. Inside I was asking, "Lord why did You bring him into our lives if You were going to just take him away? Why all the pain? But Your will be done Lord, not mine."

Two weeks later, Samuel was to go on a business trip to East Germany, but he was rerouted at the last minute to a different meeting in Atterdorn, Germany. His travel arrangements were mixed up, and he was put in first class next to a man who owned a German automotive company. As they spoke, the man told Samuel how he needed to fill an engineering manager position. The qualifications were hard to find: he had to know the German language, and preferably Italian and French, and he had to have worked in engineering in Europe and America. And the trick was that this person also had to manage his new office of engineers in an area called the northern Midwest, (which turned out to be only about 2 hours away from where we lived) in the US. How was he going to find such a person? Of course, Samuel, who had all of these qualifications, was sitting right next to this man! Further, this man was also going to Atterdorn where Samuel was headed. Samuel shared our story with him and soon they arranged for an interview. Without a problem, he was hired with a visa to come back to the US. God wanted our trust; He wanted us to know that He had arranged the union, in His way, His timing but with our obedience to Him. He called me up and excitedly told me that he was coming back so we could be together!

When Samuel came back, we decided to have a chaste relationship until we would marry. We fully realized God was calling us to be together in this holiness. We wanted God to have all our obedience, trust, and holiness, with a surrendered heart. God was giving us another one of His "Second Chances!"

CHAPTER 7

The Wedding Feast

amuel didn't formally ask me to marry him right away, though we talked about the possibility and where we would live. His new job would be two hours east from Restore and the kids' dad for that matter. It was October of 2002. His formal question about marriage would be connected with a trip to my family farm without my knowing. For as long as I can remember, my family has always had a big Thanksgiving dinner on the farm. All my aunts and uncles and cousins come. It is not something any one of us would miss. We have cribbage tournaments, great conversations, guitar playing, singing, and all the food you could ever desire from all the aunts who bring a dish to pass. So like every other year we headed out on the nine- hour drive home to my parents farm. Samuel came with us as he had the other years we had been dating. I didn't realize this happened, but on Friday after dinner with my parents, Samuel and my father went out to fix up some boards on the big red barn. Samuel had asked my dad if he could speak with him about something in private, so they went out with a tall ladder to fix one of the highest loose boards on the barn. After Dad sent him up the ladder to hammer it down, Dad asked him what he wanted to talk about. So from about twenty feet up in the freezing, wintry air

Samuel asked my dad for his blessing to marry me. I'm not sure what all they said to each other, but I didn't find out about that conversation until after Christmas.

On December 24, just as we had for the last three-and-a-half years, Samuel and I went for our yearly walk along Lake Michigan's austere winter coast, near where we had prayed about his leaving for Europe only months before. We got all bundled up and went out to the icy beach. It is like nothing you will ever see anywhere on earth. The fresh cold waves crash up against the lighthouse and its channel, freezing in big swells along the beach with the sand dunes in the distance. People walk along these icy swells looking over the strong, cold waves of Lake Michigan's endless water line. It reminds you just how vulnerable and helpless you are and how big is our God. As we were walking along the beach, Samuel stopped, knelt down, and asked me to marry him. He presented an engagement ring that meant (and still does mean) the world to me. It is a gold band with four birthstones: the two boys, mine, and his own. I was really surprised by how much thought he'd put into the ring. It was his way of saying yes to family and commitment in the most sincerely loving way I could have ever have imagined.

Inside I was hoping he would ask me during this special time. I actually almost expected it since it was our special time alone every year when the kids went to their dad's. I had asked God for a mate, for someone to help me in the journey home. He'd answered by sending me Samuel. Sometimes I felt so unworthy of this gift, like in these moments, that it didn't seem real with all I'd been through. When he knelt down in the frozen sand, part of me wanted to giggle like a schoolgirl out of nervous excitement and part of me wanted to be this mature romantic, but I was not sure how to exactly pull that off. I just tried to be myself, be quiet, and enjoy the moment.

"Yes, Samuel, I would love to be your wife." We hugged, and he swung me around in my snowmobile pants, boots, heavy coat, scarf, and hat. This was not fluffy, surreal love but real love blessed by our Father, and we felt it. With cold, red cheeks and noses, we held mittened hands and walked back to the car full of joy for what lay ahead.

We set the wedding date for October 18, 2003, in Switzerland. There were a few things we needed to work out about our move before we got married. The kids' dad was still lived nearby, so we arranged to all talk together. He had married the woman he was living with as soon as the divorce was final. They were living in a beautiful home out in the country about ten miles from where I lived. The kids went to visit them every other weekend, and so he needed to be informed about our decision to marry and move two hours east. Samuel didn't have much contact with him, yet the two seemed to have a quiet reserve toward each other that was healthy. I had learned to accept and actually be grateful for Cruz's wife, Terrie, for she loved the boys and took good care of them while they were there. Through my growth with God and healing, I had been able to forgive Cruz; the old past, in amazing grace, seemed to have melted away. This didn't mean, though, that my ex-husband had changed all his ways.

We called Terrie and Cruz and ask them if we could all sit down and discuss how the future looked concerning the move and the kids. They wanted to meet at their home after dropping off the kids for the weekend. Their dad was not at all comfortable with the move and having to drive half way to meet up with the kids. He had moved to Chicago about two years earlier for his work, and we had to drive to meet up with them half way. This had been frustrating for all of us. Now that he was back near the boys, he didn't want to do that again. The meeting got a bit heated, but we decided to discuss it further as time went on. Samuel and I prayed about it, and asked God for guidance about what we should do.

About a month later, their dad was let go from his job and later got a job offer in New York. He had to take it, having nothing else on his plate here near the boys. This meant a few things. Our move was now an open door, and the boys would be with us even on weekends, allowing Samuel to be more fully in the role of being their dad. This was another miracle of amazing grace that flowed from obedience and trust in our Father's best way.

Closed doors don't always mean they are locked, but it does mean we need to trust in God's provision, pray asking for His guidance, and then go forward in peace. I have learned that closed doors help me to stop and see if I am being self-centered or God-centered. They give me time to realign my allegiance to what God wants and His timing and to learn trust. How, when, and which of the doors open, I need to leave up to Him in obedient trust. Prayers are always answered. Maybe not in our way or timing, but they are answered in love for our best way. He was showing us that He hears even in silence.

We decided that Samuel would rent an apartment near his work for the month before the wedding. He had to fly back to Germany after that month to work for a while. This gave me time to sell our house and move us into the apartment after he left so that we'd be all together after we got back from the wedding. We had a rummage sale, put the house on the market, and prayed. No one came. It was on the market for nearly a year. I finally took it off the market and tried to sell it by owner. I learned that St. Joseph was a good saint to help sell a home, so I started asking St. Joseph to help us out. As soon as I did that the neighbor who owned the golf course our home was on called and said she was interested in buying our home. Now that I was selling it without a realtor, it would be cheaper for her and I would receive more. It was hard to finally sign the papers away from this loved home, but it was also exciting to look to our future life.

I put in my month's notice at work. That wasn't as hard as it I thought it would be. They had a nice sendoff party for me and gave us a gift certificate for an expensive kitchen store. I bought nice matching Italian spaghetti dishes with a serving dish and a waffle iron for the breakfasts I would now have time to make for the kids before school. That last day at work was not only the last day there, but my last day as a single working mother. It was also the last day I would be going out of the home to work for a long time. We had decided that I would be a stay-at-home mom, taking care of the home, yard, dinners, shopping, and cleaning. I was excited to find out what being home could mean for the first time in my life. I had always wanted to raise a family in the traditional way, but profession and life decisions had made that impossible up to now. I fully wanted to embrace this gift God was giving to me. I wanted to learn how to bake, can, and cook real dinners. I wanted to make a home for my new family that had good smells and someone always home to welcome them. I wanted to be powerful in my supporting role. Even though I didn't always admit it to myself, I was jealous of other women who could stay home and raise their families.

Even when I was a young girl with my best friend out on a walk in the back woods, after she asked what I wanted to do with my life, I had mentioned that I wanted to be a stay at home farm wife; *that* was my dream. After many years of frustration, it was coming true. Secretly in my adult life, I had wanted that so much but fought against it, and now God was even gifting me with it!

We rented a U-Haul with Billy sitting on the seat next to me carrying his favorite stuffed bear I'd given him from my past; a stuffed bear Jason had bought me when we were in college. He fell asleep, and the bear somehow slid under the seat, and we forgot about it. We lost that bear along with some of its past as we moved on. It was a big change for all of us.

We moved into a 1,100 square-foot, two bedroom, third-floor apartment. There was a pool just below our little deck on one side and a play yard with a pond on the other side outside the kids' bedroom. We loved it! We moved in late September while Samuel was in Europe, just before we flew to Switzerland for the wedding. I planned to start the kids in their new school when we got back.

The plans for the wedding were all coming together. Our best man was Sam's friend from Switzerland, and the maid of honor would be his sister. In my husband's traditions, the maid of honor and best man make the arrangements for the wedding, not the bride and groom, so you pick someone who you trust to do what you'd want done. You give them suggestions, approve of the bill, and pay it, but they do all the arrangements, right down to the flowers. We picked out the menu and the big events, but they did everything else. My job was to write a speech for the dinner, get a dress and outfits for the boys, and arrange the invitations and send them out. Sam arranged for our stay before the wedding.

To this day it amazes me that my whole family came! Even my Godmother came who never travels out of our home state. All my brothers and sisters came with their husbands, wives, and kids, except my older sister's kids and husband who couldn't work it out to come. My mother and dad's favorite number is thirteen. Everything seemed to happen on the thirteenth, including my birthday. All thirteen of them all flew together to Switzerland. Samuel's family and friends arranged a wonderful program for my family, even letting them stay in their family mountain chalets (like a cottage here in the US) while they were there. They had the time of their lives and still talk about the trip to this day.

Before we flew to Switzerland I had been praying that God would receive the glory for our wedding. I wanted Him to be glorified in the speech I gave and wanted Him to guide me in what to say. One night after praying and going to bed, I had a dream, and in the dream, God gave me the exact words to say. I remembered them when I woke and wrote them all down. It was a beautiful way to glorify him and a wonderful, fitting wedding speech for my husband and our families. I could not have written such words. Somehow on the day of the wedding, I lost the paper with the speech on it, but it all came to me without the paper. I was even able to give the last bit of it in Swiss German with the words, "Ich liebe dich, mein shatz," which means, "I love you, my treasure," as I looked at my husband with love and new hope for our lives. I could feel God's presence in those words. Many people came up to me later commenting on how it had affected them.

The wedding was truly like a fairy tale. We were married in his little hometown village, in the only church of the village, on the hill. My sisters and brothers sang a song we had picked out that have words that go like this: "Wherever you go I shall go, wherever you live so shall I live, Your people will be my people, and Your God will be my God, too." These verses about Ruth from the Old Testament really seemed to go with our story. We also sang the song, 'Amazing Grace', which, without a doubt, was perfect for God's grace in our being able to be together. As a wedding gift, my older sister gave us this song painted on papyrus. It meant the world to us. Even the neighbor farmer chipped in and was able to get two alp horn players to come to the ceremony and play old traditional songs for us that were just rich with tone, romance, and beauty. I felt God there blessing us and sending us forward as we took our candles separately and lit the one wedding candle together.

After the ceremony, we followed the Swiss tradition of cutting a log on the cobblestones in front of the church. The log, about one-and-a-half feet in diameter, is laid flat over two wooden crosses. The new spouses each take an end of a two-handled cross cut saw and saw through the log. This symbolizes life together as it could be. For example, if you make it through the whole log together that is supposed to be a sign that the marriage will last through thick and thin. The trick of this tradition is the start. You cannot saw alone, nor can you push it through. The one has to pull as the other pushes and vice-versa. The couple has to figure out a rhythm that works. The beginning and end seem to be the toughest. In the beginning you're trying to figure it out. It's hard when you hit knots in the wood, and then you get tired, for it gets long and hard past the middle. Often the man wants to do all the labor, but that just doesn't work; the wife must do her share. The whole crowd cheers you on just as family and friends should do for a couple in a marriage. We were never intended to do it alone, but with the encouragement and support of loved ones. We cut through the log without much trouble, there were those knots, but I have to say it was a relief to be cheered on to victory!

After the log cutting, we took all the guests onto rented buses for a beautiful driving tour. We stopped at an old, covered bridge along the river to take pictures. My in-laws' farm assistant and the godfather of my godson set up a dingy that Sam's sister and brother-in-law had bought for our sailboat and put it down by the riverside. They had all the guests sign the dingy to send us on our new journey. Our bus tour ended at an old village where we walked along the cobblestone streets to the little harbor to board a two-story river cruise boat for a two-hour boat trip on the Rhine River.

On the boat trip we had wine, drinks, warm cheese sandwiches, and sweets that were to die for. Everyone had a great time. We then got off the boat and boarded the buses to go to dinner waiting for us at an old castle on the top of a tall hill with vineyards all around it, called Castle Swandeg. All our guests were invited to spend the night in the castle. Samuel and I also had our own little suite that had been owned by a writer in the eighth century. It was dark as we walked up the cobblestones to the castle. My new brother-in-law David had arranged Finish Candles in the courtyard just before the stairs. This involves three or four foot logs standing on end split in a cross half way down filled with kerosene and burning like a large candle. It was truly beautiful to come to up on the hill in the dark with the stars and the castle in the backdrop. We all stopped and talked there for a bit before going in.

The hall was unspeakably beautiful. There was one very long table with chairs on either side, and running down the middle of the table was a continuous centerpiece of wild flowers picked and arranged by my nieces, sister-in-law, and mother-in-law. In the center were two gourds that had grown into what looked like swans bowing their heads toward each other. The farm neighbor had given these to my mother-in-law for the celebration. The hall had wooden floors and beautiful old paintings from the late tenth century and was lined with wonderful, large old windows. We had a fabulous four-course meal with a dessert buffet. The food was simply out of this world.

We ate, listened to speeches, and then had music and dancing. The father-daughter/ mother-son dance was special for me because it helped me feel forgiveness and acceptance from my dad.

Since Sam is an engineer, as are many of his friends from college, they set up a game for our guests to figure out in teams. It was to build a bridge that would be able to hold the weight of a five-pound gold piece. The winner got to keep the gold. My father and Sam's best friend, figured it out together. It was nice that my father was one of the ones to figure it out because he never had the opportunity to go to college but I had always thought that he had an excellent engineering mind.

The last item was a wonderful surprise. Our brother-in-law had built a framed puzzle that was two-feet square. He had sent a puzzle piece to each of our guests and asked them to paint or put art onto their piece of the puzzle that showed something of what they wanted us to see, remember, or know. The inside of the puzzle formed a wooden heart with the others holding it in place. It was special to us how each person formed their piece and how they'd spent time on their pieces in the months before the wedding. One was made backwards, and one didn't show up because of a death. Just like life, sometimes it is confusing, and sometimes we must endure the end of things or relationships. In that moment, we felt so loved by everyone's message, but the most special to me was my dad's.

Up to that point I hadn't really felt forgiven by him for my mistakes and wanderings but seeing his piece made it all melt away. He had a picture of himself with me standing by an apache helicopter with the words, "And now enter into a new page of your life. Love, Dad." God knows what we need, and I needed a cleansing of the old and acceptance from him. It is so special to receive a written letter from our fathers, something I hadn't realized I needed before that moment. What a gift this puzzle was and still is for us. I still read and look at each piece today, thinking of the author and artist and how we are each such an important part of this mosaic of life together . . . such an integral part of the whole.

The night in our suite was beautiful. After so much waiting, time we had given to the Lord, we were now ready, ready with a fullness of knowing each other more intimately. The ancient rooms were cold yet so warm. Samuel's sister had set up two dozen yellow roses over the bed spread, with wine, cheese and bread on the table by the window. Samuel was so gentle, so intimate with me. For us both, it was as if it was the first time. It was unity with each other made possible by being in God's holy way. In the morning, my siblings wanted to see our room, and my sister the artist took a picture where Samuel and I had laid my long, white satin gloves with the pearl necklace next to his cuff links on the antique wooden table. God had made our intimacy so much more beautiful than we had ever expected, and we have been blessed ever since.

The next morning we all had breakfast together in the restaurant in the lower part of the castle and then we were off to spend the day in Lucerne. The memory of those special days with my family and friends is something I will never forget, such a loving gift of forgiveness and new life given by our God to His children . . . so blessed so protected, so loved.

CHAPTER 8

Learning the Give and Take Needed in Our Earthly Marriage

*I*n the case you think I am saying this is a fairy tale ending, full of princess dresses and glass shoes, I would like to say that our marriage is a real one, full of challenges and struggles along with love and respect. I suspect this is the same as our spiritual relationship with God. There is a honeymoon, but then there is the marriage, the work of life, the dash on the tombstone between the birth and death. We work at it continuously. We invited God to our wedding, but then we needed to invite Him more than ever into our marriage.

Not only did we have a combined family from divorce with a step-parent who'd never parented before, but we came from different cultural backgrounds. We had different traditions and ways of handling things, different foods, manners, and Christian religions. With all these differences we were bound to face struggles, but God knew we would face these challenges with Him in the center. He chose to strengthen our unity and longevity not only in our marriage but for eternity.

When Samuel and I argue or don't see eye to eye, I draw strength from the fact that God brought us together in the first place. In both of our minds, there is no doubt that He blessed our marriage and placed His hand on it from the beginning. When I feel frustrated or like giving up, I say, "Marie Therese, God gifted you with this marriage. He is with you. Do not give up. Do not let the devil divide what God has put together." From this knowledge I find a peace, a well to draw on when I feel empty.

It was 2003 and just before the housing bubble exploded. Our first challenge was finding a home. We looked for a full year at homes, but everything was so expensive. We had agreed that we would buy a home that would allow us to use only a quarter of our take home pay a month toward the mortgage. We'd heard of this on a Christian radio station and it seemed to be the right thing. After praying, we came across Deuteronomy15 that showed us that creditors should release debt within seven years. So we decided this also applied to us to set ourselves up to be released from debt in the same amount of time. Further, Proverbs 12:9(RSVCE) says, "Better is a man of humble standing who works for himself than one who plays the great man but lacks bread." Oh, the realtor sharks were telling us we could easily afford a home in the $500K range. Having God's guidance and wisdom though, through prayer and His Word, kept us safe, not just then, but for when the housing market crashed years later. It was very tempting to look at those wonderful new homes. I did look at one once, but I am more than happy now that I listened to Samuel's gentle reminder of our decision. We even looked at a potential foreclosure that was only a block from the elementary school. We thought it would be perfect, though it had a small back yard and the high ceilings concerned us because of heat loss. Overall, though, we still thought it was the best we'd seen. We placed a good bid on it, the only bid the seller received that would have gotten him out of his pending trouble, but somehow he was blocked in getting back with us in time, and we were unable to buy it. This was frustrating at best. I wondered why my prayers weren't working out for that particular home.

Back to the hunt, by this time I had looked at nearly every home in the area, and nothing seemed to be coming up. Again, my patience in God's timing was being tested. I found an older healthy home built in 1976 that was for sale by owner because he had built a new home and needed the equity from that one to finish paying off the builders.

It had a big acre lot, mature pine trees in front and back with a circle drive, a brick front, a sprinkler system with lush grass, and even a lake lot association that came along with the house only a block away with a beach, sand volleyball court, boat launch, and pavilion at our disposal. The price was within one dollar of our top limit for a house to pay off in seven years. It was also still in the school district we'd chosen for the kids and close to the freeway for Samuel to get to work. I hadn't seen this house before because it wasn't for sale. Another man had put in an offer and been accepted, but his loan had not gone through, so it was up again when I drove by after the failed purchase of the foreclosure home. It was all in God's best timing. The interior was open like we liked but without cathedral ceilings. It had two-and-a-half bathrooms, three big bedrooms, an office, a big kitchen with lots of new cupboards, double oven and nice appliances, a living room of over 420 square feet, with a wonderful open view from three Anderson double sliding doors off the back of the house to a nice deck.

Samuel looked at me in awe as we walked through the house. We knew instantly it would be ours. The seller took our offer in May, rented it for three months from us while he finished his new home, and we moved in at the end of August, 2004, after painting and preparing the home to be ours.

We had been obedient and stuck to God's guidance regarding price. If we had forced a purchase before that one, we would not have gotten the "banquet" house. Seven years to the month later, we paid off the house.

I actually tried to pay it off before the seven years were up, getting over zealous in our goal. Three months before the desired time we had the rest of the money to safely pay it off, but just before putting the money in the mail, we suddenly had a large electrical problem in the house and a water softener that went out costing us nearly all the money we were going to use to pay off the house. Though frustrated, I put the house payoff on hold until the allotted time.

I realized that it had become a point of pride on my part to pay off the house early. Eventually, I became grateful for having had the money to fix the electrical problems and replace the water softener. We paid off the house in the allotted seven years that the Lord had showed us, but it was in His timing coupled with our obedience. Such freedom from following His guidance is wonderful. Especially now with the uncertain economy, we are so grateful to have listened to His safe guidance and not the worldly temptations and father of lies. We were learning about waiting for God!

With our home secured, we started to settle into our new life. At first it was like a fairy tale, but soon routine settled in. One of the prayers I have been shown by God over the years came through a Bishop who came to talk at our church. He told us, "Pray that you can be extraordinary in the ordinary," and "ask Theresa of Lisieux to pray for you in this quest." Being extraordinary in the ordinary takes fortitude and perseverance. It's easy to live life on the fast, fun track, but ordinary life takes real character because it involves suffering of all kinds. "More than that, we rejoice in our sufferings, knowing that suffering produces endurance, and endurance produces character, and character produces hope, and hope does not disappoint us" (Romans 5:3-5 RSVCE).

Soon some of the cultural differences I mentioned above started to become more evident, especially over what to eat and how to eat. It seems a little thing, but in Samuel's upbringing, things are stiffer than I was used to at the table. For him, eating is an event. He was taught you must place the fork on the left and the knife on the right with a dessert fork over the plate at the top. That you should sit straight up with the appropriate distance between yourself and the table. Elbows could not touch the tabletop, and no sounds should come from your mouth. Foods were to be nicely displayed. Not only had I been a poor, single mom of boys, but I had been a farm girl with five siblings in a busy household. Samuel had only one sibling and had been single prior to our marriage.

These differences needed to be ironed out for our newly blended family, and, in some respects, still are being worked out. Samuel would get angry at the boys if they made sounds, didn't sit up, or used their fork improperly. I hadn't been too concerned about such things before since my upbringing hadn't emphasized table manners. We were civilized, and we washed our hands before meals, but our forks were on the right so we could get to them more easily. We rarely ever used the knife to scrape food onto the fork. We just used our finger! This drove Samuel crazy. I thought he was too hard on the boys, and it caused us problems for years. It has been a give and take from both sides prefigured in our wedding cutting log ceremony. Now the boys know more manners than they would have, but Samuel has also learned how to laugh and relax at the table.

This struggle bled over into disciplining the boys in general. Many times I felt torn between supporting the boys and supporting my husband. This was the hardest struggle of all. When I felt he was too hard on them and said so, it always caused an argument between us. He felt like his authority was being questioned, which it was, and I felt the hurt in the boys as they were being yelled at for not being more refined. How could I remain silent about something I didn't fully agree with? Usually, it was "how" he corrected not "what" that I had trouble with. I wanted him to be gentler and to let some things slide, but he wanted to stick to the way he saw it without grey areas. We were both right and both wrong. I had to learn to remain silent and talk to him about it later, and he had to learn to give a little. It took a lot of prayer, frustration, and growth on both of our parts.

Samuel was in the business of raising men while I still wanted to shelter my babies. A women's heart is often softer than a man's. Children need both for a balance in the healthy guidance of growing. I had been the only one up to then, so there had been no argument. Here I was faced with new type of power struggle in my life, one I hadn't expected. These boys were not mine, they were God's, and He had given them to me for a time to help raise them. God was asking me to give up my control over them and surrender some of that to Samuel as their earthly father.

Samuel wanted the boys to have clear guidelines for chores and a quantitative way of showing that they'd accomplished their duties for the family. They had chores, but I had never structured them. I was tired of the military ways. Another source of contention was whether or not they had done their chores to a standard or just checked them off. He made them both a pegboard that they could mark off with a peg daily so that we all could see what chores had been accomplished. I was starting to feel as if I was being told that I hadn't done a good job up to then. I needed to realize that the boys were growing up and that God had sent us a man to help them make the transition to responsibility. I was frustrated, though, with how harsh Samuel was when he verbally corrected their faults. He needed to realize that they were indeed boys, not men, and that softness and gentleness in correction was needed. Again it wasn't the "what" as much as the "how" that frustrated me. "Wives, be subject to your husbands, as is fitting in the Lord. Husbands, love your wives, and do not be harsh with them. Children, obey your parents in everything, for this pleases the Lord. Fathers, do not provoke your children, lest they become discouraged" (Colossians 3:18-21 RSVCE). We were learning how to be a family, how to build character and support our family unit so that we would find hope and not discouragement. This took patience and many disagreements, even counseling at one point, but again, I would remember how God had put my marriage together and that it was in His best plan for us all.

Our spiritual lives were also changing. I became more and more involved in Bible studies, teaching, catechism, and speaking at Rite of Christian Initiation for Adults (RCIA) and other church activities. Samuel was going to mass every Sunday and some obligation days, and even went to a men's retreat. He still did not want to convert even though he did go to RCIA classes to learn more about our faith before dropping out before the conversion, and so I did not push it. This was God's timing not mine. The boys both became altar boys and were involved with catechism classes and youth group.

After realizing that the boys had to be on the list at the Catholic Church from birth to be enrolled at the Catholic school, we elected to put them into the local public school we'd chosen when we were looking for homes. The apartment had not been in the school district we'd chosen, so I had had to drive the kids the first year before moving into the house. This gave me the opportunity to talk with other moms while we waited to pick up our kids. I met many women with whom I became friends, and I joined some nondenominational Bible studies. In time I became a leader of many bible studies, including one in my own neighborhood. It was a time of growth for me in my faith.

Our Lord in His wisdom furthered our marriage by placing an opportunity in our laps one day. Sometimes Samuel had to go to Europe on business, and one time there was a large European sailboat show happening at the same time. He was elated. While there he met a man who made racing sailboats in Switzerland. He was looking for someone who could speak German, French, and English to help "launch" his new boat line in the U.S. market. Samuel is an entrepreneur. He loves new business and the hope of what it can bring. With his engineering, manufacturing, mechanical, sailing, and language experience and my open schedule, it seemed to be a good fit for us. We knew nothing about importing boats, let alone day sailing or racing. Our only sailing experience had been on our twenty-seven foot Catalina family sailboat. But when he came home, we prayed about it, and God showed us it was something He blessed, so we started the business in our home. It was truly exciting.

The business became my new job during the day. It took many hours of investigation and study to get a legal title, legal import paperwork, clearance through the Coast Guard, and a myriad of other things. We also had to find sailboat dealers on both the west and east coasts and introduce the boat by advertising and entering boat shows. Once I even flew out to the east coast to receive a boat for a customer. Upon pulling the boat out of its container, I discovered that the trailer was not wired correctly for the United States. I rewired all of the backlights of the trailer right there while the customer watched. Luckily, there was a shop nearby where I could buy what I needed to do the fix and ask needed questions. Never in a million years would I have thought I could have done that, but I did it through the grace of God. I didn't hide anything from this customer. In fact, as other issues surfaced, I brought each detail to the manufacturer's attention and worked it out so as to be fair to the customer.

When we first went to Switzerland to look over the boats and develop a contract with the manufacturer, the Lord showed us through prayer and scripture that this business would not make us money, but that it would be used by Him. Indeed, we broke even with enough money to buy a new computer, camera, and other necessary business items. Our faith was tested with difficult customers and people we worked with and for who challenged our honesty. This cost us money at the time and tested our trust in God.

Maintaining integrity at every turn, however, we were a witness to everyone we dealt with, especially our manufacturer. We worked with the leading sailing magazines and other advertisers and became really close with the people we worked with. Soon we were sharing our faith not only through our actions but through our words. I regularly prayed one of Mother Theresa's prayers, "Lord help me to love the people You send along my path today." We learned to bind together, hold firm, and trust in each other and God more and more.

We called the business SM & G, Inc. for Samuel, Marie, and God, Inc. So every time we made a call or had correspondence, we reminded ourselves that we were working with God and had to act likewise. Soon the boat we were importing became "Boat of the Year" for the whole of the United States! We were simply amazed.

God had blessed us in our work and because of this success we came in contact with certain people we believe God wanted us to get to know, that would have otherwise been impossible. We were able to go to boat shows in Annapolis and San Francisco and meet with people we read about in magazines. It was a fabulously exciting adventure.

Through time the Lord also showed us when we were done. It was hard discerning that He meant what He did, but we were convinced our time was at an end. As it says in Ecclesiastes, 3:1, 6(RSVCE) "For everything there is a season, and a time for every matter under heaven: a time to seek, and a time to lose; a time to keep, and a time to cast away." There is a time for everything, and God gave us that time to witness for Him, but it was time to let it go. I guess in heaven we will one day see what the full impact and reasons were for our involvement in that business, but I do know we had many, many chances to witness for Him.

He also helped us to build a strong trust and respect for each other in the business environment we shared as a couple. We learned how to share our ideas, celebrate and trust in each other's strengths and weaknesses, and build up a firm foundation.

In my off time, I continued doing Bible studies. God was using our whole life experience to show us His way for our marriage and to share it with all we came in contact with. In one such study I had in my home, we were studying the words *submit* in Ephesians 5:22 and *respect* in Ephesians 5:33 between husband and wife. I was struggling with these words, but I wanted to do what God was showing me. I often think of what our neighbor girl said to me one day when she was young and came over to play with the boys when they were using sidewalk chalk on the driveway. They got into an argument over which color to use where. She came up to me in the lawn while I was working and stated, "Mrs. Kceif, your boys don't knowd much. I knowd mostest, but they just don't see it." I smiled as she walked off haughtily in her self-righteousness with her bad grammar, but it always comes back to me as a reminder when I subconsciously do the same. With Samuel, I often had the "I knowd mostest" approach. Though I may have been right many times, I realized that I could still learn from others and understand how they saw things differently from me.

So I started to pray that the Lord show me where I was weak in the area of submission and respect. I found that the meaning of submission, a willingness to yield or surrender to someone, was not a weakness at all but a strength, and one that I did not possess fully. God wanted me to be strong in Him; this was just another way of showing me how to "be all I could be." While on earth, Jesus had been submissive to His heavenly Father and to others like Joseph, His earthly father. I wanted to be more like Jesus so that I could experience all the joy in my journey He meant me to have.

I am telling you; watch out what you pray for! He answers all prayer and not always how we think He will. My car started to act up. It was a Sunday night and my husband said he wanted me to take my car in to have it looked at so that he wouldn't worry about me being stranded on the side of the road somewhere someday. I had lots to do the next day: I had a leader's group meeting about a new study starting up at the Catholic Church, had to go grocery shopping, and a few other errands. I was very interested in the meeting and didn't want anything to prevent my going to it. I just couldn't fit it in. Samuel nicely suggested, "I would still like you to do it, anyway. We can drop off the car tonight at the shop and call them in the morning to have a look at it. Can't you call one of your friends to come get you for the meeting? I'll leave it up to you, whatever you want to do."

I wanted to do it when *I* wanted to, not when it was suggested. I didn't want to rely on others to give me a ride and inconvenience them. I hated to do that. Then I remembered my prayers about submission.

After thinking about it, I told Samuel that I would like to take the car in that evening.

After calling the women in the group, strangely enough, no one was home, not even the next morning. That meant I would have to ride my bike five miles to the church. It was late October and a bit cold, but it would be ok. God knew what He was doing.

After the meeting on the way home, I drove my bike past a big, old Victorian home that sat on the corner of a block in town. I had seen the home a million times before driving by in the car but never really looked at it or knew what it was. I always thought it was a private residence of a rich family. As I biked alongside the house, I looked into one of the big side bay windows. A woman, named Ethel, I'd later learn, was working on a puzzle. She looked up and waved to me with a faraway look in her eye. I smiled and waved back. The feeling left me chilled somehow. Then I heard a voice speak to me as loudly as if I were having a conversation with someone right next to me. "I want you to go in there." At first I tried to dismiss the voice as somehow my own mind. I thought, *I'm not going in that house. I don't even know a single person there. What would they think if I just went up and knocked on their door? And anyway, what would I be going in there for?* I kept riding. As I turned the corner, the big home's front was now to my right side. As I pedaled by the front of the house, another woman, named Georgia, I would learn later, simply raised a limp hand trying to wave at me silently without expression. Again I heard a voice say loudly, "I want you to go into this house."

I knew without a doubt it was the Holy Spirit speaking to me. I argued with Him, again saying to myself, *I don't know anyone in there. I don't even know what I'd say. No, I'm not going in there.* I can't believe I even thought of arguing with God . . . but I did. Thankfully, He has patience and is forgiving.

Just then I looked up to see a large bag of trash, cut open and strewn all over the sidewalk. I had to get off my bike and walk around it on the grass. *Wow, where did that come from? I didn't see that before.* As I was getting back on my bike, again I heard the voice say to me, strongly but gently, "This is your last chance. I want you to go into this house."

I began to pedal forward but then slowly leaned over, got off, and turned my bike back toward the house. *Ok Lord, I hear You. I know it's You, and I am going into that house for You. I don't have a clue what You want me to do, but I am going. At least You could give me some Girl Scout cookies or something so that I'd have a reason to appear at their door knocking.* I parked my bike on the front steps and slowly ascended to the big wooden double doors. I felt like a kid who was fulfilling a dare or something. I knocked once, twice, no answer. But I knew this did not get me off the hook. So I quietly turned the knob on the door and pushed it open slowly. It opened into a beautiful entryway with a wooden banister and winding staircase going upstairs, a parlor with overstuffed leather couches, and a big dining room full of fireplaces and large windows looking out to the sidewalk I had just been riding on. There was no one there. I looked off to the left and saw a long hallway with a ramp. As I started to walk down the ramp a woman in nurse's clothing came out and asked me if there was something she could help me with. *Ok, Lord this is Yours. You are on! Help me out here.* I came to realize that it was an assisted living place, but one that really looked like someone's personal home. In my reply all I could muster up was, "Is there someone here who could use a visit?" *Wow, Lord, that sounds kinda lame . . . but let's go with that.* She didn't even bat an eye and said, "Oh, yes, there's Georgia. She has a son, but he doesn't come often, and she would love to have someone to talk to." She simply showed me her room and left to go about her business. I was stunned. I just walked in and started talking with a woman whom I'd never met before in my life, and no one even questioned me. Later I found out that they were very conscientious about who came and went, and even had an alarm on the door, but that day God had prepared them for my coming. I spent two hours with Georgia, getting to know her and sitting with her at dinner.

After dinner, on my way out, a woman named Linda was sitting in her wheel chair waiting for a ride down the ramp. She asked me why I was there. "I really am not sure, but I felt compelled to come here," I replied. "It's a story I really can't explain. I don't have any relatives closer than nine hours away. My own grandparents have all died. I suppose I was coming to have family in a way."

She replied, "I could really use someone to come be my friend. Could you come and spend time talking with me sometime?" My heart went out to her, and I saw in that moment that God wanted me to learn how to love outside my immediate family.

All this because I had been submissive to my husband. I would have never stopped had I been in a car, with all my rebellious arguing, but on a bike, He was more able to slow me down to hear His will for me. This was a means of growth for me to reach out in love to the lonely and aged and an answer to my prayers to learn submission all in one.

Linda was fifty-seven years old when she had her stroke. She had been a Martha up until then, literally running from one job to the next. She had been a professional woman, working on her masters, giving encouraging speeches in hospitals on anxiety and stress her whole life but not realizing it in her own. She had many, many deep wounds from her past, which I suppose is what kept her own children from coming to visit her. She had had an aneurysm on the brain and went in for the surgery but had a stroke during the operation and was never the same. Now she was 66, lonely, and in need of someone to love her and treat her with the respect of a friend. She was a parishioner at the Catholic Church I had just come from and went to on the weekends. God knew we would grow together.

We have been close friends now for five years. We meet every Wednesday to work on her bulletin board, go out shopping, or simply sit and talk. It's like *Tuesdays with Morrie* only it's my own personal *Wednesdays with Linda*. I have learned a lot about loving others, praying for others, and giving outside myself simply for the love of God.

It hasn't all been easy. Sometimes giving up my time has required much patience. I also continued to meet with Georgia. She only had a few years left to live, though we did not know it then. We often talked about how God loved her, of her past on the farm, and her son. She passed away a year ago. I have seen many of my friends there come and go. It has been a real applicable Bible study of life. God was slowly showing me how He blesses obedience and how He intended me to mature in Him with His family for His Kingdom.

CHAPTER 9

Beginning Surrender in My Spiritual Marriage

round the time I met Linda, more and more questions were looming for me that were not being answered by the nondenominational bible study program in which I was enrolled. As a leader, I became increasingly worried about whose authority or interpretation was correct. Who could I turn to for answers? I decided to join the Bible studies at the Catholic Church in our town where we went on weekends. They introduced me to a book called the Catechism of the Catholic Church or CCC. In the back, I found how the Church interpreted most scripture verses. This became more and more helpful to me. No longer was I flailing around with my own interpretation. The Holy Spirit could talk to me through the Word, but now I had safe authority to go to in case I was putting selfish or ignorant twists on what I read.

I soon became a leader there. Our study had over 130 people in it broken down into small groups with a large group lecture given by a priest after the small group discussions. I flourished there and found much needed healthy friendships with women. God was introducing me, or rather reintroducing me, to my spiritual family through His church.

I started to realize that I had not surrendered to all the Catholic Church taught. I hadn't been to confession in twenty-five years. I didn't really believe that Jesus was present body and soul in the Eucharist. I wasn't comfortable with how I was supposed to relate to the Holy Virgin Mary. I hadn't gone through an annulment from my first marriage nor had my current marriage been blessed by a Catholic priest. I'd had my tubes tied . . . the list was looking really long. I didn't want to be a hypocrite, guiding a Bible study at a church in which I didn't subscribe to all it taught. I wanted answers.

The first issue I tackled was my unbelief that Jesus was present in communion at mass. So I started to pray to Jesus to show me in my soul that He was truly present in the Eucharist. It was one thing to subscribe to what the church taught, but it was another matter entirely to really believe it in my soul. I wanted to believe because I had seen through experience that His truth was alive in the Catholic Church. There were a few things God needed to show me first so that I could grasp the answer to this prayer.

That summer I went home to my parent's farm with the boys to visit. While I was there, one of my mom's best friends started to talk to me about the beauty of confession. I didn't want to listen at first, but considering my concerns about being a hypocrite, I decided I should. She said that Jesus was present in the confessional through the priest and that when I told my sins to him, Jesus was listening. He already knew what I wanted to say, but saying it out loud to His chosen representative was a way of surrendering and acknowledging all that was wrong in my life. This would allow me to receive grace to rise above temptation the next time I would face it. Indeed, it was like the prodigal coming home to Jesus who was lovingly waiting for her.

I decided to go when I got back home. How could it hurt me? So I went to church on a Saturday afternoon to see Father Harsten, a tough old farm boy who most people were afraid of. His side of the church was empty, whereas the other priest's was full. I asked the only man kneeling there, "Why aren't there any people on this side?" "Most people are afraid of the truth and of Father Harsten, he said. "But

Father Harsten is kind in the confessional. You don't have anything to worry about." I decided I needed someone who could handle what I was about to tell him. I didn't want to be let off lightly, so I stayed strong and went face-to-face with Father Harsten. After all, I wasn't doing it to check confession off a list. I was truly seeking this sacrament and its graces.

I unloaded twenty-five years of selfish rebellion. It felt like a ton of bricks came off my shoulders that day. I felt so alive and free. Not only did the past twenty-five years seem to fall away, but I had a better realization of where I was at in the present. I wanted to be rid of mediocrity and live fully, even if that meant looking at my weaknesses. I felt alive, renewed, and strengthened to do just that. Father Harsten was like Jesus to me, kind, gentle, loving, and patient to listen to twenty-five years of confession. It was a good thing that there wasn't anyone waiting in line that day!

Now I go at least once a month. The grace and power I receive from this sacrament is amazing. It fills me with so much joy and hope to be a better child of God. After coming out of church after confession the other day, even my teenage son said, "Wow, what a load off. I feel so much better!" Of course, in a mother's heart, I had to wonder what he did, but smiling, I allowed myself to trust that grace will cover his life, too.

After I received the Sacrament of Reconciliation (confession), things started to change quickly for me. I was still praying and seeking strongly to believe in Jesus in the Eucharist. The following weekend we went out to our boat, Second Chances, to do some sailing and attended mass there. That day, the priest gave his homily on the Eucharist and conveyed to me the real presence of Christ in the Eucharist. It wasn't so much the words, but God's grace flowing through the priest, my surrender to God from the Sacrament of Reconciliation, and my truly seeking His presence that enabled me to experience Jesus for the first time as being truly present. Fr. Hardon comments on the Fifth Luminous Mystery of the rosary's tenth bead: "The Mass will be fruitful in the measure of our surrender to the Father," and, "We will benefit only as much from the graces of the sacrament sacrifice of the Mass as we mirror the image of the life of Christ in our lives" (S. J. Archives; Eucharist).

I sat in the church next to my husband and boys, weeping with joy, unable to stop. My husband lovingly put his arm around me, though he didn't understand it himself. To this day, I still feel this overflowing presence of His love and holiness when I go to daily mass. It overflows in tears during His Holy Sacrament. Someone once told me that it is called the gift of tears, and now I know why.

After that weekend, I was on break at the Bible study one day when I overheard one of the older women say, "When I was younger, I went through a divorce and remarried. Since I never had an annulment, the priest suggested that I could not receive communion." I remained silent, not wanting to tell anyone, but it really bothered my soul. Should I not be going to communion now that I finally believed in Jesus as being there? Why not? The whole thing did not make sense to me. But everything that God had been showing me had been in answer to me wanting to be fully aware of the ways in which I had not yet surrendered to His ways through His church. This seemed to be following suit, so I took it as if God was speaking to me.

I went home and researched what Catholics thought about annulments and divorce. Everything seemed to be pointing to seriously putting in for an annulment. But I didn't really believe in annulments. Hadn't I gotten married? Hadn't I gotten divorced? And weren't the divorces my fault for the most part? So what did annulment mean? I called up one of my older friends from the Bible study whom I respected and trusted to keep my question confidential. She immediately told me to go talk to Father Harsten. But I really didn't want to bring this to his attention because I knew it would be a real commitment once I went in to talk with him. Not only that, but Samuel would have to be involved. But my wanting to do God's will over my own was so strong that in the end after seeking other advice, even online, I went in and spoke with Father Harsten. He told me right away that I needed to start the process. But he also told me, "Marie, you shouldn't receive communion until this annulment is final. Without the annulment, the church sees that you are still married to Jason, and therefore not in communion with the church. If you think you can, you should also not have marital relations with Samuel until the annulment is final and your marriage is blessed in the Catholic Church."

My head was reeling. Was I really hearing what he just said? I couldn't believe it. Now that I believed in His presence I was being told not to receive. And being abstinent until I got annulment was inconceivable. Father Harsten saw my frustration. In tears, I said, "Why, Father Harsten, should I stop receiving our Lord now that I see Him for the first time in my life?"

He told me gently, "You are not in communion with the church."

"I don't understand. What does being in communion with the church mean?" He quietly and patiently tried to explain. I told him, "I really think my non-Catholic husband will not understand the abstinence part either. How do I explain this to him when I don't fully understand it myself?" He told me if it was too much for me to accept that he would give me communion and to pray for God's guidance about the physical union with my husband.

I felt so heavy leaving his office that day, but I knew God was pointing me in this direction, even if I didn't understand the whole thing. I went home, prayed, and cried a lot. I remember talking it over with God and telling Him, "God, though I don't understand what You are doing right now in this annulment process, and I don't fully agree with it all, I want my will to be Your will. I will do this, but I need Your grace and help to talk with Samuel about it. Please help him to see Your will, too." I talked with Samuel that night, and to my amazement, he supported me even though he didn't understand. This was real love. This was answered prayer. It was grace at work. I was simply amazed at what God was doing.

When I went to confession the next weekend, the priest I went to told me to start frequenting adoration. Adoration, he told me, was when the priest placed Jesus in the form of the Host on the altar in a large gold container called a *monstrance*. Then the Host was exposed to the congregation to adore Him in that form. Our church held silent adoration the first Friday of the every month after 9:00 am mass until 5:00 pm. That coming Friday was the beginning of the month, so I signed up for an hour during the day in the quiet little old stone chapel. I did not expect what I found — quiet serenity. I prayed to Jesus and adored Him; He helped me understand and gave me peace. In silence, we hear Him loudest.

Soon after, I started the long process of the annulment. It took a whole year for the tribunal of the diocese to investigate. This meant a whole year of going to adoration instead of communion. One of the first weekends I was at mass was the hardest for me. It nearly broke my heart that I had to abstain from receiving communion. It was a rainy day with full cloud cover, but right in the hardest time just before everyone went up to receive, a light shone brightly through the stain glass window onto my face, warm and bright, as if to tell me, "Have peace and patience, My child, I am doing this for your best. I love you. Thank you for listening and following Me." It was a gentle hug from Jesus. I smiled and it was ok. Fr. Harsten told me that I could come up with the procession but put my arms across my chest to show that I just wanted a blessing but couldn't receive communion. Doing this helped me to feel as if I still belonged.

Meanwhile, I had to have letters from people who knew Jason and me when we were dating and could explain how we met, married, and why we divorced. I didn't know anyone anymore except my own family so I thought this part would be impossible. The church did not recognize my second marriage because we weren't married in the church, not to mention that it was by a justice of the peace in her home. The real work was with the first marriage.

At first, Jason wasn't at all open to the annulment. He was still bitter. He told the tribunal that he would not fill out the paperwork. I think he frustrated the investigator with his reply, but I understood that God was trying to help him release the hurt he had harbored for so long.

Strangely, my old roommate, who just happened to have been our maid of honor, emailed me out of the blue. I hadn't heard from her since our wedding. Now isn't that just like God? She was not a Catholic but wanted to adopt through the Catholic Church and remembered that I was Catholic. After we talked, she agreed to write a letter to the tribunal telling what she knew. I told her what happened and urged her to tell the truth as she knew it, not biased toward anyone.

Ann from the college swim team still happened to be at her old address by our old Calvary unit with the same phone number. She also agreed to write a letter with the facts. God had worked also in her life, and she was interested in what God was doing in mine. My mother also wrote a letter to the tribunal.

During this time, Jason called me because the tribunal had contacted him. At first he was frustrated with the whole thing, but what he really wanted was an apology, a healing. In the course of our long conversation, we shed many tears and even had a few laughs. This annulment process seemed to be healing not just me but those I had hurt so many years ago. They seemed to need closure, too. It was good for them to be part of the process, and it was good for me and Jason. In the end, Jason became very helpful in the annulment process and mailed out his letter.

Finally, the annulment process was complete. I was finally free to marry Samuel in the Catholic Church and have its blessings. Samuel agreed to do this. My mom and dad drove up to be witnesses to our marriage on Dec 3, 2006. Looking back, I can honestly say that I became a real advocate of the annulment process. It is yet another guide the Holy Church has given us toward unity, healing, and peace. Her ways are Jesus' hands and feet guiding us on His best and perfect way.

After the annulment other things were revealed to me that needed attention in my life. Being immersed in the church and her members I slowly came to realize that having my tubes tied was not within her teachings. Humane Vitae 14, an encyclical letter written by Pope Paul VI in 1968, says that sterilization is contraception and that it is not within the healthy guidelines of our church teaching. "Equally to be excluded, as the teaching authority of the Church has frequently declared, is direct sterilization, whether perpetual or temporary, whether of the man or of the woman" (© Libreria Editrice Vaticana; Humanae Vitae 14). I also investigated and discovered what the Church further says about it in the Catechism of the Catholic Church: "Periodic continence, that is, the method of birth regulation based on self-observation and the use of infertile periods, is in conformity with the objective criteria of morality. (HV16) These methods respect the bodies of the spouses, encourage tenderness between them, and favor the education of an authentic freedom. In contrast, 'every action which, whether in anticipation of the conjugal act, or in its accomplishment, or in the development of its natural consequences, proposes, whether as an end or as a means, to render procreation impossible'(HV14) is intrinsically evil:"(CCC2370).

The reasons our Church gives us not to perform direct sterilization are to do with freedom, integrity, self-control, and respect, not to mention physical health. These are all for our good and are holy, the opposite is evil. The more I investigated it, the more I came to see how harmful this act had been to me. Even medical research now shows women who'd had their tubes tied are exposed to higher rates of heart disease, osteoporosis, and hormonal imbalances. Based on the positive outcome of submitting to the other guidelines of the Church, I knew God was speaking to me and that I should take it seriously. Samuel had never had his own children, I wanted more, and my time clock was ticking away.

A friend from church who I'd known for about two-and-a-half years gave me a card for a doctor she'd heard about who did reversal surgery. It was so odd that she gave it to me at the same time as God was revealing this to me. I didn't talk with Samuel about it right away, but I prayed that God would prepare his heart to discuss it with me. The issue weighed heavily on my heart. It seemed that everywhere I turned, I read or heard about tubal ligations, babies, and the desire for reversals.

I decided to seriously talk to Samuel about it over Christmas break. He wasn't open to the idea at first because he was worried about me going through such a serious operation at age 40, and he wasn't sure whether or not he wanted children. He said he'd pray about it and think it over. I decided not to bring it up again, not push him, but to wait on God. I asked God, "If You really want me to go through a reversal operation, please prepare Samuel's heart to want this. I'm all in Lord, but I need Samuel's support as my husband. Please help me to follow Your way for me." A full year went by as I prayed and waited, and my desire to have the reversal grew. I started to want it more and more. Our God is so wonderfully clever. He started to put babies in front of Samuel everywhere he went. Babies, babies and more babies. Even at church, we would sit down right in back of a couple with a newborn baby. There were pictures of babies in his sailing magazines, or we would get a movie and invariably there would be a couple having a baby in the movie. He even started to hear story after story about births and newborns on the public radio station he listened to while going to work. The whole thing started to be humorous as he shared all the incidents with me. After a year of seeing babies, in October of 2007, he told me that he thought we should definitely have the surgery. He asked me to get the information from the surgeon so he could look it over.

I was elated, but it had taken almost a whole year of trusting and waiting on God to do His work. But now I had a problem; I couldn't find the card my friend had given me, and she no longer had the information.

I decided to pray to one of my favorite saints; Saint Anthony, to help me find the card. One day I was cleaning and was about to dump out a box of old letters. Out of nostalgia, I opened the box to leaf through the contents before letting it go, and right on top of the box was a St. Anthony medal with the card right underneath it! If that wasn't a sign from God and an answer to prayer, I don't know what was!

We got in touch with the surgeon, Charles Dieter, D.O., F.A.A.O.S, and found out that he was known all over the world for his wonderful work in this area, not only for women but for men. We also discovered that he worked out of Merrillville, Indiana, only about three hours away. He could have been anywhere in the nation, but he was only three hours away! Through our research, we also learned that reversal surgery can cost up to $25,000, but Dr. Dieter did his surgeries as a ministry and only charged just above his costs, including the anesthesiologist. Our total cost was only $4,800. The tubal ligation had been fully covered under my insurance right after Raphael was born, but not so for the reversal. It was so easy to stop life, and so difficult to reverse the decision, but God was helping us out, showing us the way.

We scheduled the consultations, met with the doctor, sent the needed information, and finally made the appointment for Friday December 28, 2007. The procedure was almost like a retreat for us. The doctor prayed with us before the surgery, and our nurse was a woman who had almost become a nun. They were cheerful and joyful, like family. To be honest, recovery in the first two days was no picnic. They had to move stomach muscle and had to make a three-and-a half-inch cut through the lower abdomen lining just at my underwear line. It took about three weeks for me to fully recover from the surgery. My stomach muscles could not handle lifting anything heavy the first few days. It was hard to get in and out of bed at first, but quickly I recovered, and was out driving within four days . . . which I was told not to do, but I didn't listen.

About this time I came across a program called Natural Family Planning (NFP). It was about how to read your body when it was fertile and how to either achieve pregnancy or naturally space births. I received the necessary books and started to track my temperature among other things. Samuel even started helping me, watching what God would do. Over time though I learned to leave it all in God's hands, not being discouraged monthly when I realized there was no baby yet. I learned to be joyful and grateful for what God had done and was doing in our lives despite how I thought it should be. I have given over the reins in this area also.

We are so happy that today we listened to God's guidance, though we have not yet gotten pregnant. Perhaps we were to do this only for the sake of obedience and my long-term health. We are still hopeful but are leaving it all up to our Lord. The desire in me to have another child has not dissipated, so I continue to pray and wait on the Lord. I also ask Him to take away the desire if it is not meant to be. Perhaps this book is my baby, and I am meant to wait for grandchildren. I am at peace with whatever the Lord wills in my life. I have seen that He has been right up until now. I have no reason to doubt Him.

Soon after my surgery, I took the boys out bowling one weekend. Samuel was away on business. For some reason, I got strike after strike, knocking all the pins down like I'd been practicing my whole life. Though I hadn't played in over ten years, I got a 220 my first game. One of the women who managed the bowling alley asked if I'd ever considered being on a league. I told her it just didn't seem to fit, and that I didn't know anyone whose team I could join. She told me they had a team in which none of the team members knew anyone either, and that they needed one more player. It would be on Wednesday nights. I told her I'd talk to my husband about it. I didn't really have a desire to go out for bowling, nor did I think it fit into my family's lifestyle. I was not used to the environment of smoking, drinking, and strange conversations. But when I talked to Samuel about it, he wanted me to do it. I was stunned. As I thought about it, I actually thought it would be fun, so I joined up. When I prayed about it, I asked, "God what are

You up to now? You know I wasn't out looking for this, so I guess this is You, right? Please use me as much as You can."

When I joined the team, we were seated last and least likely to win. One guy had around a 50 point average, a woman in her eighties did green apple shots while bowling, and the other guy's average was around 120. It didn't look good. But just like God, we ended up number one with the best overall score! Our eighty-year-old woman's average came up to over 200, and our guy with an average of fifty ended up in the 150s. But that wasn't why God had brought me there.

The man with the fifty average and his girlfriend who came with him had been reconsidering their Catholic Church. They were in their sixties and had had hard pasts. She had been married to a military man, divorced with one husband and through a death from another; he'd been divorced twice and also been in the military. This opened up a connection between us right off. She was in a wheelchair, having lost a lower leg to a bone disease, and he had problems reconnecting with a long lost son who had also started to bowl with us. Over time we got to know each other well, encouraged each other in our journeys of faith and even visited at each other's homes. They eventually got married in the Catholic Church, and even transferred to our church and started doing Bible studies. Eventually, they were able to buy a home in town and move out of their small trailer.

The eighty-year-old woman's daughter was dying from a bad kidney but she was unable to give her hers, and they didn't know anyone else who could donate. I wanted to give one of mine, but Samuel wouldn't see it. Her daughter eventually died, but we were able to rally around her in faith, consoling her. She or her family hadn't had much faith up to then, except one sister who I met at the funeral who'd been praying for her. She told us how much we meant to her sister and how our faith had helped her. I hadn't realized just how much just bowling together had done all that. God was showing me how to love others, how to reach the heart in me that was truly meant for prayer, giving, and, yes, even receiving His love through them.

After the bowling season came to an end, Wednesday nights became the night the kids went to their religious classes, and I went to prayer group. I loved prayer group. It was a little group of about ten people who met in a small chapel to praise and worship our Lord. He gifted some of us with the power to speak in tongues and others to interpret what was said. Many times I received guidance about something or someone He wanted me to reach out to.

I had been praying about my relationship with Jesus' mother, Holy Mary, and how the Catholic Church saw this, and how I was not fully on track with it. I wanted to honor her more, but something from my past held me back. I just couldn't make the step. My own mother had resisted honoring Mary more than the other saints, so possibly this came from my upbringing. But I wanted to know what Jesus wanted me to do.

In the prayer group, I met a man named Ron Jomeo. He loved Holy Mary and had a deep devotion to her. He would always invite me to come to his rosary sessions, and even had me lead a few decades from time to time. A decade of the rosary is a prayer said ten times; the prayer is called The Hail Mary. A person starts the decade by saying one Our Father prayer and ends with the Glory Be prayer and a small prayer that goes like this: "Oh, My Jesus, forgive us our sins and save us from the fires of hell, lead all souls to heaven, especially those most in need of Your mercy." Then you go on to the next decade. There are five decades in one rosary for each Mystery. While saying this decade, we think about the particular mysteries, or incidents in the life of our Lord and His Mother, that we are on. There are four main mysteries that help us reflect on Jesus' life and guidance for us. They are tied to the liturgical year of our church. We have days of the week we pray and reflect on each mystery. Consequently, one who recites all the mysteries reflects on the whole liturgical cycle that the Catholic Church commemorates during the course of each year.

The Four Mysteries are as follows:

1. Joyful Mystery (Annunciation, Visitation of Elizabeth, Nativity, Presentation of Jesus in the Temple, Finding Jesus in the Temple)
2. Luminous Mystery (The Baptism of the Lord, Wedding of Cana, Proclamation of Kingdom, The Transfiguration, The Institution of the Eucharist)

3. Sorrowful Mystery (Agony in the Garden, The Scourging at the Pillar, The Crowning of Thorns, The Carrying of the Cross, The Crucifixion)

4. Glorious Mystery (The Resurrection, The Ascension, The Descent of the Holy Spirit, The Assumption, The Coronation)

I had never even once said the whole rosary through like this. I knew what to do, but never having done it, I was nervous. But when I started to pray and reflect on Jesus' life, it just came naturally. He saw my struggle and gently prayed for me. Now through the rosary I learned, and continue to learn more and more, about Jesus, His life, and His guidance for me in dying to self and living in love.

Ron brought me a beautiful 8" x 11" picture of Mary he'd gotten in Medjugorje, a town located in western Bosnia and Herzegovina where it is said she appears. Ron went more than forty times. I framed it and put it up in the hallway of the upstairs at home. Every time I went by this picture, I thought about Mary and my relationship with her. But not until Ron brought a little booklet called, *In the End, My Immaculate Heart Will Triumph*, did I really start to understand Mary's role in my journey toward heaven. This book is a consecration preparation to our Holy Mother's immaculate heart so that we may learn from her how to be more and more like Jesus. I read through it daily for 34 days and started to understand for the first time how this beautiful spiritual mother would help me on my journey. It pointed me toward virtues I needed to be working with, and it provided me with scriptures and prayers that brought me closer and closer to Jesus on a daily basis. Mary was trying to help me on my journey of faith, just as my own earthly mother had when I was younger.

Ron died unexpectedly just last week while saying the rosary before 8:00 am mass. He went peacefully, quietly, while waiting and praying. Mary has shown me she is a strong help for souls in this confused world.

I felt some confusion about how best to honor Mary. I did not want to make God jealous of my devotion to her, but I wanted to honor her at the same time, just as I did my own earthly mother. I didn't know how to do this, but I knew Jesus was calling me to a deeper devotion to His mother and mine. Soon after this, I had a vision of a woman in my bedroom while I was praying. It was brief but so beautiful and peaceful. Not long after that a woman who I think was Holy Mary appeared to me one time when I took communion. She was dressing me in a beautiful white wedding dress. I couldn't even make it out it was so bright. She was preparing me to receive our Lord, not only for communion there on Sunday but for eternity.

The story of Jacob's ladder and my own dream became very heavy on my soul during this time that I mentioned in chapter three. There was something in that story that was showing me that I needed to learn the song of the angels on the ladder up to heaven, and that I indeed could. I began desiring the meaning of the songs and rungs that would progress me to Him.

A few days after going on a mini day retreat to see Father Solonas Casey's church in Detroit, I was introduced to Mary Agreda's book, *The Mystical City of God*, written by a seventeenth-century nun who had a vision of the blessed Virgin's whole life from birth to death. The book has been accepted by over ten popes as an authentic vision and as good guidance for us to read. I devoured it. She had a similar dream to mine of Jacob's ladder. Mary had explained the dream to her. The rungs were virtues, learned and practiced against vice. The songs were our praise and prayers going to heaven as we learned the way. Mary was the ladder helping us ascend toward her Son. It gave me goose bumps when I read it. Reading this chapter and Mary's interpretation was like hearing Mary speak directly to me. I knew she wanted me to work on the virtues from the pamphlet and studies, and now this, perfecting them in grace from Jesus.

Oddly enough, or should I say appropriately enough, during this same time I was introduced to a spiritual retreat focusing on virtues. My aunt who lived in Canada and with whom I had not spoken in years had been shown through prayer to contact me so I could go to this retreat near my home. So naturally I went, knowing God was again at work in my life. I loved hearing all about virtue and how to work on it in our lives. I brought the subject matter back to my church, and we started a group called Spiritual Awakenings. I had the blessings of both our priest and the Adult Formation Coordinator. We worked on a specific virtue each week that sprang out of one of the four main cardinal virtues:

prudence, justice, temperance, or fortitude. It was an amazing group. We met for three years, and it really helped to rejuvenate the faith walks of the women who came.

The dream, the book, the pamphlet of consecration, Ron's introduction to the rosary, the virtue retreat, and our Spiritual Awakenings meetings all happened during the same period of time, pointing me not only to the virtues but showing me how our blessed mother guides us on the way to holiness and being closer to Jesus. Since then I have done the consecration preparation numerous times. I see her as my spiritual mother, guiding me on toward holiness. I want to imitate her yes to Jesus and what He wants me to honor in my life. She doesn't take away from Jesus but brings us nearer to Him in virtue.

I ask her to help me with my writing, as I know she must have helped the apostles and disciples in the new church. I ask her to help me with scripture and pray for me for protection from evil and temptation. I know she is not God or the Holy Trinity, but she is honored by God because of her chosen mission in His Kingdom: "And when Elizabeth heard the greeting of Mary, the babe leaped in her womb; and Elizabeth was filled with the Holy Spirit and she exclaimed with a loud cry, 'Blessed are you among women, and blessed is the fruit of your womb!' And why is this granted me, that the mother of my Lord should come to me?'" (Luke 1:42 RSVE). Sometimes like Elizabeth, I, too, wonder at Mary visiting me, visiting all of her children, and wanting us all to love her Son. Yes, she is blessed among all women. Thank you, Mary, for helping me along the way. I so want and need holiness and the example You provide for my life.

Now that God had introduced me to the virtues with Mary's help, He was going to show me where I fought them and how that was weighing me down and enslaving me. The first was temperance. I was not in control of my eating habits. I was in my forties, five feet and six inches tall and only weighed 127 pounds. I had never been overweight or had a problem with it and had always been fit and active. But that didn't mean that I practiced temperance with my eating. I see now that is why the self in me so hated it when Samuel corrected the boys at the dinner table. It meant that I, too, had to be a better example regarding what I ate and the quantities. The more I prayed about it, the more I saw my bad habits. For example, I often didn't eat anything at all until suppertime. I was just too busy to eat. Then when supper came, I felt justified in eating all I wanted.

I have a great metabolism, but as I get older, it's not as great as it was. Lately, I have seen a butt emerge where I never really had one, and my belly has started to round out where it has always been hard and flat. But what really got my attention was the soreness I started to have in my throat after eating. Certain foods aggravated it more, and the faster I ate, the worse it became. My chest started to have a burning sensation, too. I went to our family doctor for advice. He told me that I had acid reflux and to watch what I ate, eat slower, and eat less at one time.

We were studying temperance in our Spiritual Awakening group, so as I began to see this as related to temperance and the virtue that stems off it, which is self-control, also a fruit of the Holy Spirit evident in an obedient child. I asked God to help me surrender to Him. It wasn't as easy as I thought it would be. First I surrendered in prayer, and then I studied the scriptures. The next morning after getting the doctor's diagnosis of acid reflux, God told me to not eat anything at all and that when my weight went down to 126, that would be the sign to start eating again. It was a strange suggestion from God, though up until then He hadn't steered me wrong. Still, I decided to test what I heard. 1 Thessalonians 5:21 tells us to test all spirits so that we can know for sure the evil one is not trying to mock God in some way. At the time I'd been weighing myself every day and found that I was about 127, fluctuating plus or minus three pounds depending on what time of day I weighed myself. I figured that it would only take me about half a day without eating or at least a single skipped supper to have my weight fluctuate only one pound. The problem I had was with my husband. He would notice I wasn't eating with the family and ask why, and I didn't think he would understand. So I asked God if this was from Him, and if it was, I asked that He would take care of Samuel understanding.

That afternoon Samuel called me from work and told me he had to go to Kentucky for an unexpected business trip for a few days and was sorry but he couldn't get out of it. *Wow, ok that was quick, Lord. I see this is You asking me to trust in You.* God wanted to show me something, and I was wondering what He was up to. I didn't eat a thing for three days, not a morsel, and in those three days, I felt nothing but joy and peace. I had to go to the grocery store, and I was around the aromas of restaurants that would have made most people cave, but I was filled with His grace. I actually felt joy when I smelled food cooking and praised God for the talents of the cooks and the gift of food. Not once in those three days did I feel like I needed to eat, not once.

On the night of the third day just before Samuel was to come home, I weighed myself before going to bed . . . 125.5. Just below 126. I was done, and in the morning I would eat breakfast. What I learned in those three days was that God was my provision, not food, and that I did not need to binge eat to fulfill a feeling. I also learned that I did not need to eat a ton of butter on bread, smother chocolate frosting on whatever I wanted, or throw a ton of salt on all my food. God wanted me to see His provision and the right alignment of food and other things in my life. He wanted me to see how temperance could bring me more joy in my journey. I am still amazed today when I try to fast that I cannot even go a single day without at least a little bread, but I went for three whole days without a bit of trouble. God wants us to realize His given graces, have joy in things and not be enslaved by them.

After this experience, one of my friends from the prayer group told me he'd started to pray for God's will in my life about having a child. A few months later, the Lord told him that it would not be healthy for me to have a child at that time. He told me this reluctantly, but I received it. I loved the "not at this time" part in his given statement, as it gave me hope.

This also encouraged me more to work harder on temperance with my eating and other habits. Since then, I have cut out the things that really affect me. I cut out margarine all together. Now remember, I am a farm girl who smothered margarine on everything, (should have been butter but I grew accustomed to margarine somehow). This was very hard for me and took about three weeks to give it up completely. I now eat a small, healthy breakfast with a carefully picked out cereal, fruit, and juice. I no longer skip lunch but have a healthy lunch and eat it slowly. This was also hard for me because before, if I did eat lunch, it was on the fly while doing other things. Now I actually set the table and thank God for His guidance in my eating habits.

Our boys were gaining unnecessary weight because of my habits, so what I was doing was affecting my family. I realized that the suppers I was preparing for my family were too large and not as healthy as they should be. I started making menus, shopping accordingly, and reducing the amounts. Now the boys are back on track, and I am amazed that our freshman son has really grasped the concept of healthy eating and drinking lots of water. He has slimmed down to a healthy physique and established good eating habits. We still have a long way to go and are still tempted to indulge now and then, but I no longer have the burning in my chest or throat. Most of the effects of the acid reflux are gone, or at least lessened, because I changed my habits.

Cardinal virtues are formed by habitually doing something right again and again, and in the process the opposing vice is weakened to the point where it may be overcome all together. I learned that there are seven capital sins or vices corresponding with the virtues:

1. Pride vs. Humility
2. Covetous vs. Liberality
3. Lust (impurity) vs. Chastity
4. Anger vs. Meekness
5. Gluttony vs. Temperance
6. Envy vs. Brotherly love
7. Sloth (idleness) vs. Diligence

I have experienced an internal power struggle with all of these in which the vice tried to steal my joy. In the military, my pride was weakened by the humility of allowing God into my life. I fought being covetous of status by allowing myself to liberally give love to the aged and lonely. I fought the lust of adultery and having had sex before marriage by remaining chaste before marrying Samuel and reversing my tubal ligation procedure. I have battled anger over the abuse in my previous marriage by surrendering to the Father's will in meekness. Gluttony related to food has been battled with temperance. The list goes on. The more He shows me the obvious virtue and opposing vice in my life, the more I delve into where they are not so obvious, even internal. He shows me daily where vices are weighing me down and where the tempting apple of wanting my own authority and way that I have chosen is keeping me from a fullness of joy. Every week, I still select a virtue and study it all week. I ask the Lord to show me where I am still weak and what to do about it. Invariably, I am shown what I need to work on. God is not finished with me yet. He is still speaking even today, and I am still in process, forever learning, listening, and responding, just like Brandon Heath's song, *Wait and See.* "I know God says there is hope for me yet, because God does not forget the plans He has for me!"

In all of these revelations shown to me through marriage, children, Mary, dreams, scriptures, and the pillars of the Church, God has been preparing me for the plans He has for me. He has set my feet upon sharing my story in speeches at women's conferences, retreats and through my writing. My mission here is not finished. I know I have much to battle, much to witness to for Him, and it will not always be easy, but with God's ways and guidance, I will run the race well. In surrendering to Him, I am allowing His precious blood to knit back together what was hurt and injured by vices. I am growing and healing more and more every day so that I can be more productive in His Kingdom for His glory. Samuel and I are working hard together in our marriage to become more holy individually as well as a couple growing closer and closer to heaven reflecting the marriage of Christ to His church. Our struggles are not done, but through them we continue to battle and grow well in the graces of our Lord.

I have the gift of free will, but I have learned to allow it to be guided with God's perfect guides. In the end, the difference in my life has been astounding. It is joy in the journey and life lived to the fullest, being all that I can be. I pray my dear friends that you too may be on this your personal journey with our Lord and Savior; Jesus Christ, trusting in Him to lead the dance!